我的名人书信美文

用无限温柔来感谢你

英汉对照　词汇解析　语法讲解　励志语录

张　波　编著

中国纺织出版社

图书在版编目（CIP）数据

我的名人书信美文：用无限温柔来感谢你：英文 / 张波编著 . -- 北京：中国纺织出版社，2019.4
ISBN 978-7-5180-5097-0

Ⅰ.①我… Ⅱ.①张… Ⅲ.①英语—语言读物②书信集—世界 Ⅳ.① H319.4：I

中国版本图书馆 CIP 数据核字（2018）第 116718 号

责任编辑：武洋洋　责任校对：寇晨晨　责任印制：储志伟

中国纺织出版社出版发行
地址：北京市朝阳区百子湾东里A407号楼　邮政编码：100124
销售电话：010—67004422　传真：010—87155801
http://www.c-textilep.com
E-mail:faxing@c-textilep.com
中国纺织出版社天猫旗舰店
官方微博http://www.weibo.com/2119887771
三河市延风印装有限公司印刷　各地新华书店经销
2019年4月第1版第1次印刷
开本：880×1230　1/32　印张：6.5
字数：210千字　定价：39.80元

凡购本书，如有缺页、倒页、脱页，由本社图书营销中心调换

前言

　　思想结晶改变人生命运，经典美文提高生活品位。曾几何时，一个字，触动你的心弦；一句话，让你泪流满面；一篇短文，让你重拾信心，勇敢面对生活给你的考验。这就是语言的魅力。通过阅读优美的英文短文，不仅能够扩大词汇量，掌握单词的用法，了解语法，学习地道的表达，更让你的心灵如沐春风，得到爱的呵护和情感的滋养。

　　岁月流转，经典永存。针对英语学习爱好者的需要，编者精心选取了难易适中的英语经典美文，为你提供一场丰富多彩的文学盛宴。本书采用中英文对照的形式，便于读者理解。每篇美文后都附有单词解析、语法知识点、经典名句三大版块，让你在欣赏完一篇美文后，还能扩充词汇量、巩固语法知识、斟酌文中好句，并感悟人生。在一篇篇不同题材风格的英语美文中，你总能找到引起你心灵共鸣的一篇。

　　读一本新书恰似坠入爱河，是场冒险。你得全身心地投入进去。翻开书页之时，从前言直至封底你或许都知之甚少。但谁又不是呢？字里行间的只言片语不总是正确的。

　　有时候你会发现，人们自我推销时是一种形象，等你在深入了解后，他们就完全变样了。有时故事的叙述流于表面，朴实的语言，平淡的情节，但阅读过半后，你却发觉这本书真是出乎意料的妙不可言，而这种感受只能靠自己去感悟！

阅读之乐，腹有诗书气自华；阅读之美，活水云影共天光。阅读可以放逐百年孤独，阅读可以触摸千年月光。阅读中有眼前的收获，阅读中也有诗和远方。

　　让我们静下心来感受英语美文的温度，在英语美文中仔细品味似曾相识的细腻情感，感悟生命和人性的力量。

编者
2018年6月

目录

01 Leonardo da Vinci to the Duke of Milan
达·芬奇致米兰大公书 ·· 001

02 Samuel Johnson to Lord Chesterfield
萨缪尔·约翰逊致切斯特菲尔德大人 ································ 007

03 Letter to a Young Friend by Benjamin Franklin
本杰明·富兰克林给年轻朋友的一封信 ····························· 013

04 Napoleon Bonaparte to Josephine
拿破仑·波拿巴致约瑟芬 ·· 017

05 George Washington to Colonel Nichola
乔治·华盛顿致尼古拉上校 ·· 021

06 Victor Hugo to Adele Foucher
维克托·雨果致阿黛尔·富歇尔 ······································ 026

07 Friedrich Nietzsche to Richard Wagner
弗里德里希·尼采致理查德·瓦格纳 ································ 034

08 John Keats to Percy Bysshe Shelley
约翰·济慈致珀西·比希·雪莱 ······································ 039

09 Ralph Waldo Emerson to Walt Whitman
拉尔夫·瓦尔多·爱默生致沃尔特·惠特曼 ······················· 044

10 Benjamin Disraeli to Thomas Carlyle
本杰明·迪斯雷利致托马斯·卡莱尔 ································ 048

11 Abraham Lincoln to John D. Johnson
亚伯拉罕·林肯致约翰·约翰斯顿 ···································· 053

12 Abraham Lincoln to Mrs. Lydia Bixby
亚伯拉罕·林肯致莉迪亚·毕克斯比夫人 ·························· 058

13 Charles Darwin to R. W. Darwin
查尔斯·达尔文致罗伯特·达尔文 ················ 062

14 Henry David Thoreau to Ralph Waldo Emerson
亨利·大卫·梭罗致拉尔夫·瓦尔多·爱默生 ············ 067

15 Theodore Roosevelt to Theodore Roosevelt Jr.
西奥多·罗斯福致小西奥多·罗斯福 ················ 073

16 David Hume to Adam Smith
大卫·休谟致亚当·斯密 ······················ 078

17 Adam Smith to William Strahan
亚当·斯密致威廉·斯特拉恩 ···················· 082

18 Francis Scott Fitzgerald to Ernest Hemingway
弗朗西斯·斯科特·菲茨杰拉德致欧内斯特·海明威 ·········· 087

19 Adam Smith to David Hume
亚当·斯密致大卫·休谟 ······················ 092

20 Joseph Priestley to His Neighbours of Birmingham
约瑟夫·普利斯特里致邻居伯明翰 ·················· 098

21 Thomas Jefferson to Giovanni Fabbroni
托马斯·杰斐逊致吉奥凡尼·法布罗尼 ················ 105

22 Thomas Jefferson to Martha Jefferson
托马斯·杰斐逊致玛莎·杰斐逊 ···················· 110

23 Robert Southey to Charlotte Brontë
罗伯特·骚塞致夏洛特·勃朗蒂 ···················· 116

24 Charles Lamb to S. T. Coleridge
查尔斯·兰姆致塞·泰·柯勒律治 ·················· 125

25 Michael Faraday to Sarah Barnard
迈克尔·法拉第致萨拉·巴纳德 ···················· 132

26 Percy Bysshe Shelley to John Keats
珀西·比希·雪莱致约翰·济慈 ···················· 135

27 Abraham Lincoln to Miss Grace Bedell
亚伯拉罕·林肯致格蕾丝·比德尔小姐 ················ 140

28 Charles Darwin to W. D. Fox
查尔斯·达尔文致威廉·福克斯 ·················· 143

29 Alfred Tennyson to Queen Victoria
阿尔弗雷德·丁尼生致维多利亚女王 ·············· 147

30 Charles Dickens to Wilkie Collins
查尔斯·狄更斯致威尔基·柯林斯 ················ 151

31 Charlotte Brontë to Emily Brontë
夏洛特·勃朗特致艾米莉·勃朗特 ················ 156

32 Mark Twain to W. D. Howells
马克·吐温致威廉·迪安·豪威尔斯 ··············· 161

33 Eugene O'Neil to Beatrice Ashe
尤金·奥尼尔致比阿特丽丝·阿希 ················ 166

34 William James to His Students
威廉·詹姆斯致他的学生 ······················· 171

35 Charlotte Brontë to Ellen Nussey
夏洛特·勃朗特致爱伦·纳西 ···················· 175

36 Edgar Allan Poe to Sarah Helen Whitman
埃德加·爱伦·坡致萨拉·海伦·惠特曼 ············ 180

37 William Cullen Bryant to Sarah S. Bryant
威廉·卡伦·布莱恩特致萨拉·布莱恩特 ············ 183

38 George Gordon Byron to the Hon. Augusta Byron
乔治·戈登·拜伦致奥古斯塔·拜伦阁下 ············ 188

39 George Gordon Byron to William Harness
乔治·戈登·拜伦致威廉·哈尼斯 ················· 193

01 Leonardo da Vinci to the Duke of Milan
达·芬奇致米兰大公书

My Excellency,

Having, most illustrious lord, seen and considered the experiments of all those who pose as masters in the art of inventing instruments of war, and finding that their inventions differ in no way from those in common use, I am **emboldened**, without prejudice to anyone, to solicit an appointment of acquainting your Excellency with certain of my secrets.

1. I can construct bridges which are very light and strong and very portable, with which to pursue and defeat the enemy; and others more solid, which resist fire or assault, yet are easily removed and placed in position; and I can also burn and destroy those of the enemy.

2. In case of a siege I can cut off water from the trenches and make **pontoons** and **scaling ladders** and other similar **contrivances**.

3. If by reason of the elevation or the strength of its position a place cannot be bombarded. I can demolish every fortress if its foundations have not been set on stone.

4. I can also make a kind of cannon

显贵的大公阁下：

我对那些冒充作战器械发明家的人所进行的试验做了观察和思考，发现他们发明的东西与平常使用的并无两样，故此斗胆求见阁下，以便面呈机密，但对他人不抱任何成见。

一、我能建造轻便、坚固、搬运便利的桥梁，可在追逐和击败敌军时派上用场；也能建造坚固的桥梁，能经受住敌军的炮火和进攻，这种桥梁装卸非常方便；我也能焚毁、破坏敌军的桥梁。

二、在围攻城池之际，我能从战壕中切断水源，还能制造浮桥、云梯和其他类似设备。

三、一个地势太高，或坚不可摧，因而无法用炮火轰击的据点，只要它的地基不是用石头筑的，我能摧毁它的每一个碉堡。

四、我还能制造一种既轻便又易于搬运的大炮，可用来投射小石块，犹似下冰雹一般，其中喷出的烟雾会使敌军惊慌失措，因而遭受沉重损

which is light and easy of transport, with which to hurl small stones like hail, and of which the smoke causes great terror to the enemy, so that they suffer heavy loss and confusion.

5. I can noiselessly construct to any prescribed point **subterranean** passages either straight or winding, passing if necessary underneath trenches or a river.

6. I can make armored wagons carrying artillery, which shall break through the most **serried** ranks of the enemy, and so open a safe passage for his infantry.

7. If occasion should arise, I can construct cannon and mortars and light **ordnance** in shape both ornamental and useful, and different from those in common use.

8. When it is impossible to use cannon I can supply in their **stead** catapults, **mangonels**, **trabocchi**, and other instruments of admirable efficiency not in general use—In short, as the occasion requires I can supply infinite means of attack and defense.

9. And if the fight should take place upon the sea I can construct many engines most suitable either for attack or defense and ships which can resist the fire of the heaviest cannon, and powders or weapons.

10. In time of peace, I believe that

失，并造成巨大混乱。

五、我能在任何指定地点挖掘地道，无论是直的或弯的，不出半点声响，必要时可以在战壕和河流下面挖。

六、我能制造装有大炮的铁甲车，可用来冲破敌军最密集的队伍，从而打开一条向敌军步兵进攻的安全通道。

七、在必要情况下，我能建造既美观又实用的大炮、迫击炮和其他轻便军械，不同于通常所使用的。

八、不能使用大炮时，我能代之以弹弓、投石机、陷阱和其他效果显著的器械，非通用器械所能比——总之，必要时我能提供不胜枚举的进攻和防御器械。

九、倘若在海上作战，我能建造多种极适于进攻和防守的器械，也能制造可以抵御最重型火炮炮火的兵船以及各种火药和武器。

十、在太平年代，我能营造公共建筑和民用房屋，还能疏导水源，自信技术决不次于他人，而且包您满意。

此外，我还善于用大理石、黄铜或陶土雕塑；在绘画方面，我也绝不逊色于当今任何一位画家，无论他是谁。

此外，我还愿意承担雕

Leonardo da Vinci to the Duke of Milan

达·芬奇致米兰大公书

I can give you as complete satisfaction as anyone else in the construction of buildings both public and private, and in conducting water from one place to another.

I can further execute sculpture in marble, bronze or clay, also in painting I can do as much as anyone else, whoever he may be.

Moreover, I would undertake the commission of the bronze horse, which shall **endue** with immortal glory and eternal honor the auspicious memory of your father and of illustrious house of Sforza.

And if any of the aforesaid things should seem to anyone impossible or impracticable, I offer myself as ready to make trial of them in your park or in whatever place shall please your Excellency, to whom I commend myself with all possible humility.

塑铜马的任务，它将为您已故的父亲和声名显赫的斯福尔扎家族增添不朽的光彩和永恒的荣誉。

如果有人认为上述任何一项办不到或不切实际的话，我愿随时在阁下花园里或您指定的其他任何地点实地试验。谨以无限谦恭之忱向阁下推荐我本人。

单词解析 Word Analysis

embolden [ɪmˈbəʊldən] *vt.* 鼓励，使有胆量

例 Emboldened by the wine, he went over to introduce himself to her.
他借酒壮胆，走上前去向她做自我介绍。

pontoon [pɒnˈtuːn] *n.* 浮码头；浮桥平台

例 Military engineers hurriedly constructed a pontoon bridge across the river.
工程兵在河上匆匆地架设浮桥。

scaling ladder ['skeɪlɪŋ;'lædə(r)] 云梯

例 Here is an opening door. Welcome you all who are getting down from the scaling ladder of real life.
这里，是一个打开的门，欢迎所有从生活的云梯上下来的人。

contrivance [kən'traɪvəns] *n.* 发明；发明物

例 The film is spoilt by unrealistic contrivances of plot.
这部电影被不实际的牵强情节给毁了。

subterranean [ˌsʌbtə'reɪnɪən] *adj.* 地下的

例 London has 9 miles of such subterranean passages.
伦敦像这样的地下通道有9英里长。

serried ['serid] *adj.* （指士兵的行列等）密集的，靠紧的

例 Above the bush the trees stood in serried ranks.
荆棘之上耸立着密密麻麻的大树。

ordnance ['ɔːdnəns] *n.* 大炮；军械（如弹药、军车等）

例 Shoes and clothing for the army were scarce, and ordnance supplies were scarcer.
军队很缺鞋和衣服，武器供应就更少了。

stead [sted] *n.* 代替

例 Foxton was dismissed and John Smith was appointed in his stead.
福克斯顿被解职，受命接替他的是约翰·史密斯。

mangonel ['mæŋɡənel] *n.* 投石机，军用射石机

例 Manginel was widely used in ancient wars.
在古代战争中，投石机被广泛使用。

trabocchi *n.* [意大利语]陷阱

例 Watch out the trabocchi!
小心陷阱！

endue [ɪn'djuː] *vt.* 授予，赋予（特性、才能等）

例 He prayed to God to endue him with wisdom.
他祈求上帝赋予他智慧。

语法知识点 Grammar Points

① **Having, most illustrious lord, seen and considered the experiments of all those who pose as masters in the art of inventing instruments of war, and finding that their inventions differ in no way from those in common use, I am emboldened, without prejudice to anyone, to solicit an appointment of acquainting your Excellency with certain of my secrets.**

这个句子中主干为"I am emboldened...my secrets","Having seen and considered..."和"finding..."是动词的现在分词形式做原因状语。

例 Having no great talents, he lived a normal but happy life.
他没有什么才华，度过了平淡且幸福的一生。

② **If by reason of the elevation or the strength of its position a place cannot be bombarded, I can demolish every fortress if its foundations have not been set on stone.**

这是一个主从复合句，if引导了一个条件状语从句，用来说明事情发生的条件。

例 If there is no Einstein, the scientific world will be very different.
如果没有爱因斯坦，科学世界会变得十分不同。

③ **I can noiselessly construct to any prescribed point subterranean passages either straight or winding, passing if necessary underneath trenches or a river.**

这个句子中有一个插入语成分——if necessary，意为"如果必要的话"，同时也是if it is necessary的缩写。

例 He said he would help Lisa out of debt if necessary.
他说必要的时候会帮助丽莎摆脱债务。

④ **When it is impossible to use cannon I can supply in their stead catapults, mangonels, trabocchi, and other instruments of admirable efficiency not in general use.**

这个句子中有一个句型"it is impossible/possible/likely/unlikely (for somebody) to do something"，意为"某人做某事是可能的/不可能的"。

例 It is possible for you to enter a good university if you work hard.
只要你努力，就有可能上一所好大学。

经典名句 *Famous Classics*

1. There is no royal road to learning.
   书山有路勤为径，学海无涯苦作舟。

2. He who seize the right moment, is the right man. — Goethe
   谁把握机遇，谁就心想事成。——歌德

3. Cease to struggle and you cease to live. — Thomas Carlyle
   生命不止，奋斗不息。——卡莱尔

4. You have to believe in yourself. That's the secret of success. — Charles Chaplin
   人必须有自信，这是成功的秘密。——卓别林

5. The unexamined life is not worth living. — Socrates
   浑浑噩噩的生活不值得过。——苏格拉底

6. Living without an aim is like sailing without a compass. — John Ruskin
   生活没有目标，犹如航海没有罗盘。——罗斯金

7. "It is not our abilities that show what we truly are, it is our choices." — *Harry Potter and the Chamber of Secrets*
   决定我们成为什么样人的，不是我们的能力，而是我们的选择。——《哈利·波特与密室》

8. Work hard! Work will save you. Work is the only thing that will see you through this. — *Sleepless in Seattle*
   努力工作吧！工作能拯救你，埋头苦干可令你忘记痛楚。——《西雅图不眠夜》

02 Samuel Johnson to Lord Chesterfield
萨缪尔·约翰逊致切斯特菲尔德大人

My Lord,

I have been lately informed, by the **proprietor** of The World, that two papers, in which my Dictionary is recommended to the public, were written by your lordship. To be so **distinguished** is an honour which, being very little accustomed to favours from the great, I know not well how to receive, or in what terms to acknowledge.

When, upon some slight encouragement, I first visited your lordship, I was overpowered, like the rest of mankind, by the **enchantment** of your address, and could not forbear to wish that I might boast myself Le vainqueur du vainqueur de la terre;— that I might obtain that regard for which I saw the world contending; but I found my attendance so little encouraged, that neither pride nor modesty would suffer me to continue it. When I had once addressed your Lordship in public, I had exhausted all the art of pleasing which a **retired** and **uncourtly** scholar can possess. I had done all that I could; and no man is well pleased to have his all neglected, be it ever so little.

伯爵大人：

近日从《世界报》馆主得知，该报刊所载有关拙著词典之推荐文章二篇，均出自勋爵阁下手笔。承蒙您如此的推崇，本应是一种荣耀，只可惜在下自来无缘得到王公大人的青睐，所以真不知道该如何来领受这份荣耀，也不知道该用些什么言辞来聊表谢意。

回想当年，偶受他人怂恿，首次拜访大人阁下。我像所有的人一样，深为大人的言谈丰采所倾倒，不禁心生奢望有朝一日能口出大言"吾乃天下征服者之征服者也。"——虽知此殊荣是举世学人所欲得，仍希望有朝一日能侥幸获取。然而我很快发现自己的趋走逢迎皆不奏效。不管是出于自尊也好，自矜也好，我反正无法再周旋下去。我本是一个与世无争、不善逢迎的书生，但那时我也曾用尽平生所学的阿谀奉承的言辞，当众赞美过阁下——却终究不能取悦于你。能做的一切我都做了。如果一个人在这方面付出的一切

Seven years, my lord, have now passed, since I waited in your outward rooms, or was **repulsed** from your door; during which time I have been pushing on my work through difficulties, of which it is useless to complain, and have brought it, at last, to the **verge** of publication, without one act of assistance, one word of encouragement, or one smile of favour. Such treatment I did not expect, for I never had a patron before.

The shepherd in Virgil grew at last acquainted with Love, and found him a native of the rocks.

Is not a **patron** my lord, one who looks with unconcern on a man struggling for life in the water, and, when he has reached ground, **encumbers** him with help? The notice which you have been pleased to take of my labours, had it been early, had been kind; but it has been delayed till I am indifferent, and cannot enjoy it: till I am solitary, and cannot impart it; till I am known, and do not want it. I hope it is no very cynical **asperity** not to confess obligations where no benefit has been received, or to be unwilling that the public should consider me as owing that to a patron, which Providence has enabled me to do for myself.

Having carried on my work thus far

努力（不管是多么微不足道）受到完全的忽视，他是绝不会感到舒服的。

伯爵大人，从我第一次候立于贵府门下，或者说被您拒于门外时算起，已经过去7年。7年多来，我一直苦苦地撑持着我的编撰工作。个中滋味，不说也罢。所幸我的劳作而今终于快要出版，在这之前我没有获得过一个赞助的行为，一句鼓励的话语，一抹称许的微笑。如此殊荣实出意料，因为我从来不曾得到过他人的赞助与恩惠。

维吉尔笔下的牧童最后终于和爱神相识，却发现所谓爱神竟是铁石心肠之人。

伯爵阁下，有的人眼见落水者在水中拼命挣扎而无动于衷，等他安全抵岸之后，却才多余地伸出所谓援手，莫非这就叫赞助人吗？大人而今忽有雅兴来关照在下的劳作，这原本是一桩美意，只可惜太迟了一点儿。迟到得我已经意懒心灰，再无法快乐地消受；迟到得我已经是孤身一人，无法与家人分享；迟到得我已经名闻海内，再不需阁下附丽张扬。我既然本来就没有得到过实惠，自然无须感恩；既然是上帝助我独立完成这桩大业，我自然不愿让公众产生错觉，似乎我

with so little **obligation** to any favourer of learning, I shall not be disappointed though I should conclude it, if less be possible, with less; for I have been long wakened from that dream of hope, in which I once boasted myself with so much exultation.

My Lord,
Your lordship's most humble,
Most obedient servant,
Sam. Johnson

曾受惠于某一赞助人。但愿这么说还不至于太尖酸刻薄。

既然我的工作进行至今从未得到过学界任何资助,所以值此完工之际,也不会担心得到的资助变少(何来"变少"无从谈起),因为我早就已经从那个赞助的美梦里幡然猛醒;曾几何时,我还在那梦中得意非凡地自诩是大人。

伯爵阁下
您最谦恭温顺的仆人
萨缪尔·约翰逊

单词解析 Word Analysis

proprietor [prəˈpraɪətə(r)] *n.* 所有人,业主
- He was the sole proprietor with total management control.
  他是唯一业主,掌握全部管理权。

distinguished [dɪˈstɪŋgwɪʃt] *adj.* 著名的;卓越的
- It seems such a pity that a distinguished and honored name should be commercialized in such a manner.
  一个著名的、令人尊敬的名字被人用得如此商业化,似乎太让人遗憾了。

enchantment [ɪnˈtʃɑːntmənt] *n.* 魅力;迷人之处
- It was a place of deep mystery and enchantment.
  这是一个极其神秘和迷人的地方。

retired [rɪˈtaɪəd] *adj.* 与世隔绝的;遁世隐居的
- The play starred a well-known retired actress who was intent on a come-back.
  该剧由一名志在复出的著名隐退女演员主演。

uncourtly [ʌnˈkɔːtlɪ] *adj.* 无礼的；不典雅的；不会奉承的

例 He is regarded by the royal family as uncourtly and misbehaved.
皇室认为他举止失当，行为无礼。

repulse [rɪˈpʌls] *vt.* 击退；拒绝；驳斥；憎恶

例 I was repulsed by the horrible smell.
这种可怕的气味让我恶心。

verge [vɜːdʒ] *n.* 边，边缘；界限

例 He was on the verge of tears.
他差点儿哭了出来。

patron [ˈpeɪtrən] *n.* 赞助人，资助人

例 Frederick the Great was the patron of many artists.
腓特烈大帝是许多艺术家的赞助人。

encumber [ɪnˈkʌmbə(r)] *v.* 妨碍；阻碍；拖累

例 The police operation was encumbered by crowds of reporters.
警方的行动被成群的记者所妨碍。

asperity [æˈsperəti] *n.* （尤指语言、态度）粗暴，严厉

例 I said, with some asperity, that that was no concern of mine.
我颇为粗暴地说，那跟我毫无关系。

obligation [ˌɒblɪˈɡeɪʃn] *n.* 债务；义务，责任

例 You are under no obligation to buy anything.
你不必非买什么东西不可。

语法知识点 *Grammar Points*

① **To be so distinguished is an honour which, being very little accustomed to favours from the great.**

这个句子中有一个固定搭配"be accustomed to something / doing something"，意为"习惯于做某事"。

例 My father is accustomed to walking his dog every morning.
我的爸爸习惯了每天早上去遛狗。

② **When, upon some slight encouragement, I first visited your lordship, I was overpowered, like the rest of mankind, by the enchantment of your address.**

这个句子中"upon some slight encouragement"做原因状语，"upon + n."为固定用法，表示"出于……原因"。

例 Upon great fear, he dared not to enter that dark cave.
因为极度害怕，他不敢进入那个黑漆漆的山洞。

③ **But I found my attendance so little encouraged, that neither pride nor modesty would suffer me to continue it.**

这个句子中有一个固定用法"find+something+v.过去分词"，意为"发现某事被做"，也可将something替换为oneself，意为"发觉某人自己处于……状态"。

例 Five minutes later, I found myself lost in the city.
五分钟后，我发现自己在城市里迷路了。

④ **I had done all that I could.**

这个句子中could后省略了do，原因是前面的"had done"出现了动词"do"，所以从句中为免累赘，省去了动词do。

例 Don't worry, he will do all he can to help us.
别担心，他会尽他所能帮助我们的。

经典名句 Famous Classics

1. Enjoy your own life without comparing it with that of another. — Marquis de Condorcet, Philosopher
享受自己的生活，不要和别人比较。——马奎斯·孔多塞(哲学家)

2. The man who has made up his mind to win will never say "impossible". — Bonapart Naploeon, French emperor
凡是决心取得胜利的人是从来不说"不可能的"。——拿破仑

3. I'm a slow walker, but I never walk back.
我走得不快，但决不走回头路。

4. The world breaks everyone, and afterward many are strong at the

broken places. — Ernest Hemingway
这世界会打击每一个人,但经历过后,许多人会在受伤的地方变得更强大。——欧内斯特·海明威

5. Faith is what gets you started. Hope is what keeps you going. Love is what brings you to the end. — Mother Mary Angelica
信念使你启身,希望让你坚持,爱带你到达终点。——安琪拉卡修女

6. You got to put the past behind you before you can move on. — *Forrest Gump*
你只有忘记以往的事情,才能够继续前进。——《阿甘正传》

7. Difficult circumstances serve as a textbook of life for people.
困难坎坷是人们的生活教科书。

8. Better to light one candle than to curse the darkness.
与其诅咒黑暗,不如点亮蜡烛。

读书笔记

03 Letter to a Young Friend by Benjamin Franklin
本杰明·富兰克林给年轻朋友的一封信

June 25, 1745

My Dear Friend,

I know of no Medicine fit to **diminish** the violent natural **inclinations** you mention; and if I did, I think I should not communicate it to you. Marriage is the proper **remedy**. It is the most natural state of man, and therefore the state in which you are most likely to find solid happiness. Your reason against entering into it at present, appears to me not well-founded. The **circumstantial** advantages you have in view by postponing it, are not only uncertain, but they are small in comparison with the thing itself, the being married and settled.

It is the man and woman united that makes the complete human being. separate, she wants his force of body and strength of reason; he, her softness, sensibility and **acute discernment**. Together they are more likely to succeed in the world. A single man does not have nearly the value he would have in that state of union. He is an incomplete animal. He resembles the odd half of a

我亲爱的朋友：

我不知道有哪种药物能治你所提及的那强烈的自然本能；而且，即便我知道，我也不该告诉你。婚姻就是最好的灵药，这是人类最自然的状态，你也能从中找到真正的幸福。你讲的那些不结婚的理由在我看来基本站不住脚。你认为的推迟结婚的优势只是视情况而定的、不确定的，与结婚成家比起来微不足道。

只有男人和女人结合起来，人类才是完整的：女人需要男人的强健体魄和理性的大脑，男人需要女人的温柔细腻和敏锐的直觉。因此当男人和女人联合起来，就能够无往不胜。没有成家，他就不会拥有全部的人生价值，像是残缺不全的动物，像是少了半边的剪刀。

如果你有幸找到一位持家有方、身体健康的妻子，你在事业上的勤奋进取加上她在生活上的理财有道，必定会创造

pair of scissors.

If you get a **prudent**, healthy wife, your industry in your profession, with her good economy, will be a fortune sufficient.

    Your affectionate friend,
      Benj. Franklin

殷实的财富。

你亲爱的朋友
本杰明·富兰克林
1745年6月25日

单词解析 Word Analysis

diminish [dɪˈmɪnɪʃ] *v.* 减少，缩减，减小

例 His influence has diminished with time.
随着时间的推移，他的影响已不如从前了。

inclination [ˌɪnklɪˈneɪʃn] *n.* 倾向；爱好

例 She had neither the time nor the inclination to help them.
她既没有时间也不愿意帮助他们。

remedy [ˈremədi] *n.* 补救办法；治疗法

例 There are a number of possible remedies to this problem.
这个问题有许多可能采取的解决办法。

circumstantial [ˌsɜːkəmˈstænʃl] *adj.* 视情况而定的；与特定情况有关的

例 Their problems were circumstantial rather than personal.
他们的困难是环境而非个人所致。

acute [əˈkjuːt] *adj.* 敏锐的；有洞察力的

例 He is an acute observer of the social scene.
他是个敏锐的社会现状观察者。

discernment [dɪˈsɜːnmənt] *n.* 识别能力；洞察力

例 He shows great discernment in his choice of friends.
他选择朋友很有眼光。

prudent [ˈpruːdnt] *adj.* 审慎的；慎重的；精明的

例 It might be more prudent to get a second opinion before going ahead.
行动之前再征求一下意见也许更为慎重。

Letter to a Young Friend by Benjamin Franklin
本杰明·富兰克林给年轻朋友的一封信 03

语法知识点 Grammar Points

① **The circumstantial advantages you have in view by postponing it, are not only uncertain, but they are small in comparison with the thing itself.**

这句话中有一个并列短语词组"not only... but also...",表示"不仅……而且……",其中"also"可以省略。

例 Tom Chopin is not only beautiful, but also has good manners.
汤姆·肖宾不仅长得漂亮,而且很有礼貌。

② **It is the man and woman united that makes the complete human being.**

这句话中用到了一个强调句句型"it is... that...","is"后可接一个句子中的任意成分,表示强调。

例 It is at night that we watch TV together.
只有在晚上我们才一起看电视。

③ **A single man has not nearly the value he would have in that state of union.**

这是一个复合句,包含了一个定语从句"he would... union",修饰"value",定语从句的引导词应为"that/which",但因为"value"在从句中做"have"的宾语,故可以省略。

例 This is not the answer my teacher wants.
我的老师想要的不是这个答案。

经典名句 Famous Classics

1. By all means marry, if you get a good wife, you'll be happy, if you get a bad one, you'll become a philosopher. — Socrates
不管怎么说还是结婚吧,娶到好老婆,你会幸福;娶到坏女人,你将会成为哲学家。——苏格拉底

2. The course of true love never did run smooth. — Shakespeare
真正的爱情之路永不会是平坦的。——莎士比亚

3. Whatever our souls are made of, his and mine are the same. —

Emily Bronte

不论我们的灵魂是什么做成的,他的和我的是一模一样的。——艾米莉·勃朗特

4. If you live to be a hundred, I want to live to be a hundred minus one day so I never have to live without you. — Milne
   假如你的寿命是100年,那我希望自己活到100岁的前一天,因为那样我的生命中每天都有你。——米尔恩

5. A successful marriage requires falling in love many times, and always with the same person. — Mignon McLaughlin
   一个成功的婚姻需要恋爱很多次,而且始终是与同一个人恋爱。——米杨·麦克劳克林

6. Marriage is about sticking up for your partners, even when you don't agree with him. — *Modern Family*
   婚姻的意义在于,即使不认同也要支持你的伴侣。——《摩登家庭》

7. Life is one fool thing after another whereas love is two fool things after each other. — Oscar Wilde
   人生就是一件蠢事追着另一件蠢事而来,而爱情则是两个蠢东西追来追去。——奥斯卡·王尔德

8. We don't love qualities, we love persons; sometimes by reason of their defects as well as of their qualities. — Jacques Maritain
   我们爱的不是优点,我们爱的是人,有时是因为他们的缺陷,附带着他们的优点。——雅克·马里坦

读书笔记

04 Napoleon Bonaparte to Josephine
拿破仑·波拿巴致约瑟芬

Verona, November 13rd, 1796

I don't love you, not at all; on the contrary, I **detest** you. You're a naughty, **gawky**, foolish Cinderella. You never write me, you don't love your own husband; you know what pleasure your letters give him, and yet you haven't written him six lines, **dashed off** casually!

What do you do all day, Madam? What is the affair so important as to leave you no time to write to your devoted lover? What affection **stifles** and puts to one side the love, the tender constant love you promised him? Of what sort can be that marvelous being, that new lover who absorbs every moment, **tyrannizes** over your days, and prevents your giving any attention to your husband? Josephine, take care! Some fine night, the doors will be broken open and there I'll be.

Indeed, I am very **uneasy**, my love, at receiving no news of you; write me quickly four pages, pages full of agreeable things which shall fill my heart with the pleasantest feelings. I

我不爱你,一点儿也不;相反,我讨厌你——你是个淘气、腼腆、愚蠢的姑娘。你从来不给我写信,你不爱你的丈夫;你明知你的信能给他带来莫大的快乐;然而,你却连六行字都没给他写过,即使是心不在焉、草草写的也好啊。

夫人,你一天到晚干些什么呢?什么事这么重要,竟使你忙得没有时间给你忠诚的爱人写信呢?是什么样的恋情扼杀排挤了你答应给他的爱情呢?你那脉脉柔情而忠诚不渝的爱呢?那位奇妙的人物,你那位新情人,究竟是个什么样的人物,竟能占去你的每一分钟,霸占你每天的光阴,不让你稍稍关心一下你的丈夫呢?约瑟芬,留神点,说不定哪个美丽的夜晚,我就会破门而入的!

说真的,我的爱人,得不到你的讯息,使我坐立不安。立刻给我写上四页信来,四页充满甜蜜话语的信,我将感到

hope before long to crush you in my arms and cover you with a million kisses as though beneath the **equator**.

       Bonaparte

无限快慰。希望不久我将把你紧紧搂在怀中，吻你亿万次，烈火般炽热。

       波拿巴
   1796年11月13日于维洛那

单词解析 Word Analysis

detest [dɪ'test] *vt.* 憎恶，嫌恶，痛恨

例 Jean detested being photographed.
琼非常讨厌拍照。

gawky ['gɔːki] *adj.* 迟钝的，笨拙的

例 Ten years ago he was a gawky teenager.
10年前，他是个看似粗笨的少年。

dash off 匆忙完成

例 I must dash off some letters before I leave.
我必须在离开之前把这几封信给赶出来。

stifle *v.* 扼杀；压制

例 His hand shot to his mouth to stifle a giggle.
他赶紧捂住嘴，不让自己笑出声来。

tyrannize ['tɪrənaɪz] *v.* 欺压；专横（或暴虐）地对待

例 He used to tyrannize his younger brother.
他过去常常欺压自己的弟弟。

uneasy [ʌn'iːzi] *adj.* 焦虑的；不安的

例 Richard was uneasy about how best to approach his elderly mother.
该如何去跟年迈的母亲谈，理查德心里没有数。

equator [ɪ'kweɪtə(r)] *n.* 赤道

例 Singapore is near the equator.
新加坡位于赤道附近。

语法知识点 *Grammar Points*

① You know what pleasure your letters give him.

这句话中"what"引导一个宾语从句,在这个从句中"what pleasure"做"give"的宾语。

例 You have no idea what experiences he has gone through.
你对他经历的事情一无所知。

② What is the affair so important as to leave you no time to write to your devoted lover?

这句话中有一个词组"so + adj. + as to",意为"(如此……)以至于"。

例 One should learn from past mistakes so as to avoid falling into the same old trap again.
要从过去的错误中吸取教训,以免重蹈覆辙。

③ I hope before long to crush you in my arms and cover you with a million kisses as though beneath the equator.

这是一个并列句,"to crush you in my arms"和"cover you with... equator"并列,是动词不定式做宾语的情况。此外,第二个分句中"cover"前省略了"to",以免重复。

例 They are all allowed to sing and dance.
他们都被允许唱歌和跳舞。

经典名句 *Famous Classics*

1. It is possible to learn more of a human being in one minute of love than in months of observation. — Roman Rolland
   要了解一个人,相恋一分钟可能胜过观察几个月。——罗曼·罗兰

2. The hunger for love is much more difficult to remove than the hunger for bread. — Mother Teresa
   对爱的渴望要比对面包的渴望更难消除。——特蕾莎修女

3. Love sought is good ,but given unsought is better. — William Shakespeare

追求得到的爱情固然美好，但不经追求而得到的爱情更为美好。——莎士比亚

4. How on earth are you ever going to explain in terms of chemistry and physics, so important a biological phenomenon as first love. — Albert Einstein
究竟怎么用化学和物理来解释初恋这种重要的生物现象呢？——爱因斯坦

5. Some of us get dipped in flat, some in satin, some in gloss. But every once in a while you find someone who's iridescent, and when you do, nothing will ever compare. — *Flipped*
有的人浅薄，有的人金玉其表败絮其中。有一天，你会遇到一个彩虹般绚烂的人，当你遇到这个人后，会觉得其他人都只是浮云而已。——《怦然心动》

6. If you can hold something up and put it down, it is called weight-lifting; if you can hold something up but can never put it down, it's called burden-bearing. Pitifully, most of people are bearing heavy burdens when they are in love. — *If Only*
举得起放得下的叫举重，举得起放不下的叫负重。可惜，大多数人的爱情，都是负重的。——《如果能再爱一次》

7. Love makes man grow up or sink down. — *500 Days of Summer*
爱情，要么让人成熟，要么让人堕落。——《和莎莫的500天》

8. Good love makes you see the whole world from one person while bad love makes you abandon the whole world for one person. — *Jeux d'enfants*
好的爱情是你通过一个人看到整个世界，坏的爱情是你为了一个人舍弃世界。——《两小无猜》

05 George Washington to Colonel Nichola
乔治·华盛顿致尼古拉上校

Newburgh May 22nd 82

Sir,

With a mixture of great surprise & astonishment I have read with attention the **sentiments** you have submitted to my **perusal**—Be assured Sir, no occurrence in the course of the War, has given me more painful sensations than your information of there being such ideas existing in the Army as you have expressed, and I must view with **abhorrence**, and **reprehend** with **severity**—For the present, the communication of them will rest in my own bosom, unless any further **agitation** of the matter, shall make a disclosure necessary.

I am much at a loss to **conceive** what part of my conduct could have given encouragement to an address which to me seems big with the greatest mischiefs that can befall my country. If I am not deceived in the knowledge of myself, you could not have found a person to whom your **schemes** are more disagreeable–At the same time in justice

上校阁下：

认真读过您的来信后，信中这种思想态度令我大为惊骇——您放心，先生，经您确认军中确实存在的这种想法是自开战以来最令我痛苦的。我对此只有痛心之至，严厉遣责——现在我可以对此事守口如瓶，除非有人继续挑事，让我不得不把它公之于众。

我到底做了什么能让您给我写这样一封在我看来于国家利益有损的信呢？这让我百思不得其解。如果我对自己的认识没有差错，那么您不会找到比我更不同意这一阴谋的人了——同时为证明我对这一阴谋的痛恨之情，我必须补充一点，没有人比我更想看到军队里各项事宜都足够公平，只要我在政府里的权力和影响力有所扩大，我将抓住一切机会，不遗余力地推进军队公平。因此我恳求您，如果您还有一丝为国家的考虑——就算不为国

to my own feeling I must add, that no man possesses a more sincere wish to see ample justice done to the Army than I do, and as far as my powers & influence, in a constitutional way extend, they shall be employed to the utmost of my abilities to effect it, should there be any occasion— Let me **conjure** you then, if you have any regard for your country—concern for yourself or **posterity** –or respect for me, to banish these thoughts from your mind, and never communicate, as from yourself, or anyone else, a sentiment of the like nature.

家，为自己和子孙后代的考虑——抑或是对我的尊重的话，就请不要再这么想了。不论是你或是别人，都请不要再传播这种想法了。

With esteem I am Sir

Yr. Most Obed Ser

G. Washington

尊敬的阁下，

为您效劳的，

乔治·华盛顿

1782年5月22日于纽堡

单词解析 Word Analysis

sentiment ['sentɪmənt] *n.* （基于情感的）观点，看法

例 This is a sentiment I wholeheartedly agree with.
这种态度我完全赞同。

perusal [pə'ruːzl] *n.* 熟读，精读

例 On perusal, we found that part of the contents did not conform to the original contract.
经过审查，我们发现部分内容与原合同不符，请修改。

abhorrence [əb'hɒrəns] *n.* 厌恶；憎恨

例 They are anxious to show their abhorrence of racism.
他们急切地想要表明自己对种族主义的憎恨。

reprehend [,reprɪ'hend] *vt.* 斥责，指责

例 If you do not behave yourself in class, you would be reprehended by our teacher.
如果你在课堂上不守规矩的话，老师会斥责你的。

severity [sɪ'verətɪ] *n.* 严重；严格

例 The new drug lessens the severity of pneumonia episodes.
新药减轻了肺炎发作时的痛苦。

agitation [,ædʒɪ'teɪʃn] *n.* 焦虑不安；忧虑；烦乱

例 He made no attempt to disguise his agitation.
他毫不掩饰自己的焦虑不安。

conceive [kən'siːv] *v.* 想象；认为；想出

例 The ancients conceived the earth as afloat in water.
古人认为地球飘浮在水里。

scheme [skiːm] *n.* 计划；体系；阴谋

例 They would first have to work out some scheme for getting the treasure out.
他们首先得想个法子把财宝取出来。

conjure ['kʌndʒə(r)] *vt.* 用魔术变出；祈求，恳求

例 I conjure you not to betray your country.
我恳求你不要出卖国家。

posterity [pɒ'sterətɪ] *n.* 子孙；后裔

例 Two of his works have been handed down to posterity.
他有两部作品传世。

语法知识点 Grammar Points

① Be assured Sir, no occurrence in the course of the War, has given me more painful sensations than your information of there being such ideas existing in the Army as you have expressed.

比较级的否定相当于最高级，句子中"no occurrence... has given me more painful sensations than your information of..."相当于"your information of... has given me the most painful sensations"。

> He claims that nothing is more important to a country than its own benefits.
> 他声称，对一个国家而言，没有什么比利益更重要。

② **I am much at a loss to conceive what part of my conduct could have given encouragement to an address which to me seems big with the greatest mischiefs that can befall my Country.**

句子中的"could have given encouragement to..."表示"本能够……"，属于虚拟语气，对未发生但有很大可能发生的事情表示遗憾。

> When recalling his school days, he always said that he could have studied harder to get a higher mark.
> 当回想起学校生活时，他总说自己本来能再努力一点得到更高的成绩的。

③ **At the same time in justice to my own feeling I must add, that no man possesses a more sincere wish to see ample justice done to the Army than I do.**

这个句子中"done to the Army than I do"是动词过去分词做宾语补足语的用法，一般与使役动词"have、get、make"、表感觉和心理状态的动词"hear、see、notice、watch、feel、find"等词搭配，句型为"动词+somebody/ something + done"。

> On arriving at home, I find my room broken into.
> 我一回到家就发现我的房间被闯入了。

经典名句 Famous Classics

1. True patriotism doesn't exclude an understanding of the patriotism of others. — Queen Elizabeth II
   真正的爱国主义不排斥对于其他人的爱国主义的理解。——伊丽莎白女王二世

2. Old soldiers never die, they just fade away. — General Douglas MacArthur

George Washington to Colonel Nichola
乔治·华盛顿致尼古拉上校 05

老兵永远不死，只是凋零。——麦克阿瑟

3. Try to let you in the heart that one called the spark of conscience never extinguished. — George Washington
要努力让你心中的那朵被称为良心的火花永不熄灭。——乔治·华盛顿

4. The worth of the state, in the long run, is the worth of the individuals composing it. — John Stuart Mill
国家的价值，从长远来看，是个人的价值。——约翰·穆勒

5. One meets its destiny on the road he takes to avoid it. — *Kong Fu Panda*
往往在逃避命运的路上，却与之不期而遇。——《功夫熊猫》

6. True friendship is a plant of slow growth, and must undergo and withstand the shocks of adversity before it is entitled to that appellation. — George Washington
真正的友谊是一种缓慢生长的植物，必须经历并顶得住逆境的冲击，才无愧于友谊这个称号。——乔治·华盛顿

7. Hold yourself to the same standards as you hold your staff. — *House of Cards*
律人要先律己。——《纸牌屋》

8. A belief is not merely an idea the mind possesses; it's an idea that possesses the mind. —Robert Oxton Bolton
信仰不只是一种受头脑支配的思想，它也是一种可以支配头脑的思想。——罗伯特·奥克斯顿

读书笔记

06 Victor Hugo to Adele Foucher
维克托·雨果致阿黛尔·富歇尔

Friday evening, March 15, 1822

After the two delightful evenings spent yesterday and the day before, I shall certainly not go out tonight, but will sit here at home and write to you. Besides, my Adele, my adorable and adored Adele, what have I not to tell you? O, God! For two days, I have been asking myself every moment if such happiness is not a dream. It seems to me that what I feel is not of earth. I cannot yet **comprehend** this cloudless heaven.

You do not yet know, Adele, to what I had resigned myself. Alas, do I know it myself? Because I was weak, I fancied I was calm; because I was preparing myself for all the mad follies of despair. I thought I was courageous and resigned. Ah! Let me cast myself humbly at your feet, you who are so grand, so tender and strong! I had been thinking that the utmost limit of my devotion could only be the sacrifice of my life; but you, my generous love, were ready to sacrifice for me the **repose** of yours.

Adele, to what follies, what

在度过昨夜和前夜两个愉快的夜晚之后，我今晚当然就不出去了，决定坐在家里写信给你。再说了，我深爱着的、可爱的阿黛尔啊，我有多少事要告诉你啊！啊，上帝啊！两天来，我无时无刻不在问自己这样的快乐是不是一场梦境。对我而言，这种感觉简直不似在人间。这万里无云的天堂让我心醉神迷。

阿黛尔，你还不知道我卑微到了什么地步吧。唉，我自己又知道吗？因为我太过软弱，所以我佯装镇定；因为我准备好了做绝望时做的傻事，所以我自以为我是勇敢的、顺天知命的。啊！就让我匍匐在你的脚下吧，你是如此高贵、如此温柔却又如此坚强！我一直以为我为爱能做到的极致就是牺牲自己的生命；但是你啊，我的爱人，却准备好了要为我放弃你的安宁。

阿黛尔，在这漫长的八个日夜里，你的维克托什么样愚

delirium, did not your Victor give way during these everlasting eight days! Sometimes I was ready to accept the offer of your admirable love; I thought that if pushed to the last **extremity** by the letter from my father, I might realize a little money, and then carry you away—you, my **betrothed**, my companion, my wife—away from those who might want to disunite us; I thought we would cross France, I being nominally your husband, and go into some other countries which would give us our rights. By day we would travel in the same carriage, by night sleep under the same roof. But do not think, my noble Adele, that I would have taken advantage of so much happiness. Is it not true that you would never have done me the dishonor of thinking so? You would have been the object most worthy of respect, the being most respected, by your Victor; you might on the journey have even slept in the same chamber without fearing that he would have alarmed you by a touch, or even have looked at you. Only I should have slept, or watched wakefully in a chair, or lay on the floor beside your bed, the guardian of your repose, the protector of your slumbers. The right to defend and to watch over you would have been the only one of a husband's rights that

蠢疯狂的事情没想过啊！有时我都准备好接受你给我的高尚的爱了；我想过，要是父亲的来信把我们逼到绝路，我可能会想法子弄一笔钱，然后和你远走高飞——你，我的未婚妻、我的伴侣和我的妻子——离开那些想要拆散我们的人；我想，名义上我是你的丈夫，我们可以穿越法国去其他国家，在那里我们可以得到我们的权利。白天我们就同乘一辆马车上路，夜里就同在一个屋顶下睡觉。但是，我高贵的阿黛尔啊，不要以为我会趁此幸福时刻动歪脑筋。你不会把我想得这么不堪的，不是吗？你是最值得尊敬的人，是你的维克托最尊重的人；你甚至可以和他同睡一间房，不必担心他会触碰你或看着你而使你受惊。我只会在椅子上睡觉或者警觉地守卫着你，或躺在你床边的地板上，守护你的安宁，保卫你的睡眠。在牧师将作为丈夫能够行使的别的权利赐给他之前，你的仆人维克托想要的只有一个——保卫和看护妻子。

噢，阿黛尔！在坚强和圣洁的你面前，我太过软弱和卑微，请不要因此而嫌弃我，鄙视我。想一想我的损失、我的寂寞和我从父亲那里所期

your slave would have aspired to, until a priest had given him all the others...

Adele, oh! Do not hate me, do not despise me for having been so weak and **abject** when you were so strong and so **sublime**. Think of my **bereavement**, of my loneliness, of what I expected from my father; think that for a week I had looked forward to losing you, and do not be astonished at the extravagance of my despair. You—a young girl—were admirable. And indeed, I feel as if it would be flattering an angel to compare such a being to you. You have been privileged to receive every gift from nature; you have both **fortitude** and tears. Oh, Adele, do not mistake these words for blind enthusiasm – enthusiasm for you has lasted all my life, and increased day by day. My whole soul is yours. If my entire existence had not been yours, the harmony of my being would have been lost, and I must have died — died inevitably.

These were my meditations, Adele, when the letter that was to bring me hope or else despair arrived. If you love me, you know what must have been my joy. What I know you may have felt, I will not describe.

My Adele, why is there no word for this but joy? Is it because there is no power in human speech to express such

待的吧；想一想整整一周我都在担心我会失去你吧，希望我巨大的绝望和悲伤不会惊吓到你。你，一个妙龄女子，是值得被爱的。事实上，把天使和你相比，我都觉得是对天使的恭维。你是造物者的宠儿，有大自然能给予的所有美好的东西，既韧如磐石又柔情似水。噢，阿黛尔，不要将这些话误认为是盲目的热情——对你的热情贯穿于我的生命始终，并且随着时间的流逝只会增加不会减少。你就是我的灵魂的全部。如果不是为你而活，我的生命早就是不完整的、支离破碎的了，那么我一定已经死去了，这不可避免。

当我收到那封可能带来希望抑或绝望的信件时，阿黛尔，我所想的就是这些。如果你爱我的话，你会知道我当时有多么高兴。我就不详细描写你的感受了，因为我知道。

我的阿黛尔啊，为什么对此除了喜悦再没有别的词了呢？是因为人类的语言不够强大来表达这样的幸福吗？

从悲伤难过一下子跃为无尽的幸福，好像让我有点不知所措。甚至现在我还有点心神不宁，有时会兴奋得发抖，生怕从这场美梦中醒来。

happiness?

The sudden bound from mournful resignation to infinite **felicity** seemed to upset me. Even now I am still beside myself and sometimes I tremble lest I should suddenly awaken from this dream **divine**.

Oh, now you are mine! At last you are mine! Soon — in a few months, perhaps, my angel will sleep in my arms, will awaken in my arms, will live there. All your thoughts at all moments, all your looks will be for me; all my thoughts, all my moments, all my looks, will be for you! My Adele!

And now you will belong to me! Now I am called on earth to enjoy **celestial** felicity. I see you as my young wife, then a young mother, but always the same, always my Adele, as tender, as adored in the chastity of married life as in the virgin days of your first love—Dear love, answer me—tell me if you can conceive the happiness of love immortal in an eternal union! And that will be ours some day...

My Adele, no obstacle will now discourage me, either in my writing or in my attempt to gain a pension, for every step I take to attain success in both will bring me nearer to you. How could anything now seem painful to me? Do not think so ill of me as to believe

啊，现在你是我的了！终于，你是我的了！不久以后，可能是几个月，我的天使就会在我的怀中入睡，在我的怀中醒来，永远在我的怀中生活了。你每时每刻想的都是我，眼神看向的也是我；而我全部的想法、全部的时刻、全部的眼神都是为了你！我的阿黛尔！

现在你将属于我！现在我这个凡夫俗子要被召唤去天堂享受幸福了。我把你看作是我年轻的妻子，接着是年轻的妈妈，但都是一样的，你永远是我的阿黛尔，无论是在情窦初开的少女时期还是纯洁的婚后生活中，你都一样的温柔可人——亲爱的，回答我——告诉我你能不能想象得出在永恒的结合中不朽的爱情所带来的幸福！有一天我们就会拥有这种幸福……

我的阿黛尔啊，没有什么障碍能阻挠我，不论是在写作还是争取国家年金的道路上，因为在这两条道路上我为了成功而迈出的每一步都使我离你更近。现在怎么可能还有让我痛苦的事情呢？我请求你，不要把我想得那么差，不要相信还有让我痛苦的事情。如果一件事情能带来这么多的幸福，那么一点点苦痛又算得

that, I implore you. What is a little toil, if it conquers so much happiness? Have I not a thousand times implored heaven to let me purchase it at the price of my blood? Oh! How happy I am! How happy I am going to be!

Adieu, my angel, my beloved Adele! Adieu! I will kiss your hair and go to bed. Still I am far from you, but I can dream of you. Soon perhaps you will be at my side. Adieu, pardon the delirium of your husband who embraces you, and who adores you, both for this life and another.

了什么呢？难道我不是向上帝千千万万遍地祈求，让我以血的代价换来这幸福吗？啊！我真是太幸福了！我将变得多么幸福啊！

再见，我的天使，我挚爱的阿黛尔！再见！我要吻你的发丝然后再去睡觉。虽然我离你很远，但我可以在梦里见到你。也许很快你就会在我身边了。再见了，原谅你的丈夫的胡言乱语吧，他的怀抱包围着你，他今生今世、生生世世地爱着你。

1822年3月15日，星期五晚

单词解析 Word Analysis

comprehend [ˌkɒmprɪˈhend] *vt.* 理解，领会

例 My younger brother read the story but did not comprehend its meaning.
我弟弟读了那个故事，但不理解故事的意义。

repose [rɪˈpəʊz] *n.* 休息，安眠，宁静

例 He insisted on being provided instantly with a place of refuge, and means of repose.
他坚持要马上有一个安身之处和供他休息的设备。

delirium [dɪˈlɪriəm] *n.* 神志不清；说胡话

例 Robin and Nash began to show symptoms of delirium.
罗宾和纳什已经显出精神错乱的症状来了。

extremity [ɪkˈstreməti] *n.* 极端；（身体的）末端，手脚

例 I should hate and despise myself if I desert the brave warrior in his present extremity.
假如我抛弃了这位现在处于困境的勇士，我将痛恨和蔑视我自己。

Victor Hugo to Adele Foucher
维克托·雨果致阿黛尔·富歇尔

betrothed [bɪ'trəʊðd] *adj.* 订了婚的
例 Paul sent a dozen roses to his betrothed.
保罗派人送给未婚妻一打玫瑰。

abject ['æbdʒekt] *adj.* 卑鄙的，下贱的
例 He is almost abject in his respect for his father.
他对他父亲的尊敬几乎是低声下气。

sublime [sə'blaɪm] *adj.* 庄严的，雄伟的
例 Bob raised his two hands to heaven with an expression of resignation and sublime gratitude.
鲍伯带着一种听天由命和崇高的感激的表情举手向天。

bereavement [bɪ'ri:vmənt] *n.* 丧亲之痛
例 When Maria died Andy did not share her brother's sense of bereavement.
玛丽亚去世后，安迪并没有像她弟弟那样哀痛。

fortitude ['fɔ:tɪtju:d] *n.* 坚韧，刚毅
例 The long sufferings have only made him a nation of fortitude and perseverance.
深重的灾难，铸就了他百折不挠、自强不息的品格。

felicity [fə'lɪsəti] *n.* 幸福；喜悦
例 Lolita is my superior in all the charm and all the felicity it gives.
洛丽塔比我强，具有温柔的心灵所赋予的百般魅力和幸福。

divine [dɪ'vaɪn] *adj.* 神圣的；天赐的
例 The prince has renounced his divine nature and origins.
这个王子放弃自己神圣的天性和血统。

celestial [sə'lestiəl] *adj.* 天的，天空的
例 Gravity governs the motions of celestial bodies.
万有引力控制着天体的运动。

语法知识点 *Grammar Points*

① **After the two delightful evenings spent yesterday and the day before, I shall certainly not go out tonight, but will sit here at home and write to you.**

这个句子中有一个"not... but..."的连词结构，表示"不是……而是……"。

例 It was raining outside that morning, so he did not go jogging, but go swimming.
那天早上外面在下雨，所以他没有去慢跑，而是去游泳。

② **I thought that if pushed to the last extremity by the letter from my father, I might realize a little money, and then carry you away.**

这个句子中的"if pushed to the..."是条件状语从句，其中省略了"I were"。"if"引导的条件状语从句中如果主语与主句主语相同，动词为be动词，则可省略从句中的主语和be动词。

例 If admitted into Peking University, I will have the chance to meet excellent people.
如果我能被北京大学录取，我就会有机会结交很优秀的人。

③ **And indeed, I feel as if it would be flattering an angel to compare such a being to you.**

这个句子中"as if"引导一个表语从句，其中用"would + 动词原形"表示虚拟语气，与将来事实相反。除"would"外，还可用"could/ might + 动词原形"，表示虚拟。

例 He talks as if he could win the girl's heart back.
他说话的语气就好像他能把那个女孩的心赢回来似的。

经典名句 *Famous Classics*

1. Love is a vine that grows into our hearts.
   爱是长在我们心里的藤蔓。

2. If I had a single flower for every time I think about you, I could walk forever in my garden.

Victor Hugo to Adele Foucher
维克托·雨果致阿黛尔·富歇尔

假如每次想起你我都会得到一朵鲜花,那么我将永远在花丛中徜徉。

3. It is impossible to love and to be wise. — Francis Bacon
   爱令智昏。——弗朗西斯·培根

4. A friend is a present which you give yourself. — R.L.Stevenson
   朋友是你送给自己的一份礼物。——斯蒂文森

5. The supreme happiness of life is the conviction that we are loved. — Victor Hugo
   生活中最大的幸福就是,坚信有人爱着我们。——维克托·雨果

6. Born not to hold the chains, but to spread its wings. — Victor Hugo
   人生下来不是为了抱着锁链,而是为了展开双翼。——维克托·雨果

7. It is the time you have wasted for your rose that makes your rose so important. — *The Little Pince*
   你在你的玫瑰花身上耗费的时间使得你的玫瑰花变得如此重要。——《小王子》

8. Love, is not finding a perfect person, but by learning the perfect vision, appreciate that imperfect person. — *Howl's Moving Castle*
   爱,不是寻找一个完美的人,而是学会用完美的眼光,欣赏那个并不完美的人。——《哈尔的移动城堡》

读书笔记

07 Friedrich Nietzsche to Richard Wagner
弗里德里希·尼采致理查德·瓦格纳

In sending you this book, I place my secret in the hands of you and your noble wife with the greatest confidence and assume that is now your secret. I wrote this book; in it I have revealed my innermost views upon men and things and for the first time, have traveled around the entire **periphery** of my thoughts. This book was a great consolation to me at the period full of **paroxysms** and misery and it never disappointed me when all else failed to **console** me. I think it not improbable that I am still living just because I was able to write such a book.

I was obliged to resort to a **pseudonym** for several reasons; in the first place, because I did not wish to **counteract** the effect of my earlier works, and secondly because this was my only means of preventing a public and private **befouling** of my personal dignity (something I am no longer able to endure on account of the state of my health) and finally and chiefly, because I wish to make possible a scientific discussion in which all of my intelligent friends could take part, unrestrained by

这本书中包藏了我的秘密，因此我寄赠此书给你和你高贵的夫人也就是出于信任将秘密交到了你们手中，现在它也是你们的秘密了。是我写了这本书，在其中我披露了我内心深处对人对物的看法，也是第一次全面地探索了我的思想。在我情绪失控和饱受折磨的日子里，这本书对我是莫大的安慰，当所有其他都不能安慰我时，它总不会让我失望。我想，就算说我写了这本书才让我存活至今，也不是不可能的。

有很多原因让我不得不使用笔名。首先，我不愿对早期作品形成冲击；其次，这是我唯一不在公开或私人场合受到诽谤的办法了（由于身体状况我已无力承受）；最后，也是最重要的，我想制造一场科学大讨论，让我有智慧的朋友们都来参加，不受情面的约束。至今为止，无论我何时发表作品，朋友们都碍于情面不肯发言或写文章反驳我！

我认识的人里面没有人持有书中这样的观点，坦白讲，

Friedrich Nietzsche to Richard Wagner
弗里德里希·尼采致理查德·瓦格纳

feelings of delicacy, as has hitherto been the case whenever I have published anything. No one will speak or write against my name!

I know of no one of them who entertains the ideas expressed in this book and must confess to a great curiosity as to the counter arguments which such a book will provoke.

I feel very much like an officer who has stormed a **breastwork** despite his severe wounds; he has reached the top and unfurled his flag, and notwithstanding the terrifying spectacle by which he is surrounded, experiences much more joy than sorrow.

Although I know of no one who shares my views, as I have already said, I am **conceited** enough to think that I have not thought individually but collectively. I have the most curious feeling of solitude and multitude; of being a herald who has hastened on in advance without knowing whether the band of knights is following or not—in fact, whether they are still living.

我也很好奇这本书会激起怎样的异议。

我感觉自己就像一个身负重伤却以猛烈之势攻下了敌军工事的军官，冲上最高点挥舞着大旗，尽管周围的景象惨不忍睹，内心的喜悦却远胜于痛苦。

虽然我说过没有人与我有同样的观点，我还是自信地认为我的观点不是个人思考所得，而是集体智慧的结晶。我对独处和群居的感觉非常罕见，就像自己是一个先驱在前冲锋，却不知道后面的骑士们是否跟随着自己，事实上，甚至不知道他们是否还活着。

单词解析 Word Analysis

periphery [pəˈrɪfəri] *n.* 边缘；周围；外围

例 The sociological study of religion moved from the centre to the periphery of sociology.
宗教的社会学研究从社会学的中心学科变成了边缘学科。

paroxysm ['pærəksɪzəm] *n.* 突然发作，发作

例 Brian, who had watched with sincere pity the young man's paroxysm of grief, approached him.
布莱恩怀着深深的同情怜悯注视着这悲痛欲绝的青年，走到他的身边。

console [kən'səʊl] *vt.* 安慰，慰问

例 She felt she could console the child better than anyone else.
她认为自己比任何人都能更好地安慰这孩子。

pseudonym ['su:dənɪm] *n.* 假名，化名，（尤指）笔名

例 Eric Blair wrote under the pseudonym of George Orwell.
埃里克·布莱尔用乔治·奥威尔这个笔名写作。

counteract [ˌkaʊntər'ækt] *vt.* 抵消；中和

例 My husband has to take several pills to counteract high blood pressure.
我丈夫不得不吃几片药来降压。

befoul [bɪ'faʊl] *vt.* 弄脏，诽谤

例 He is reluctant to see his families befouled by mean neighbours.
他不愿意看到家人被刻薄的邻居们诽谤。

breastwork ['brestˌwɜ:k] *n.* （临时性的）低矮防护墙，胸墙

例 In the burning village I was visible to everyone and as soon as I dove into one of the trenches, the shell exploded on the breastwork.
我所在的位置敌我双方都能看到，当我要跑进一个战壕的时候，一发炮弹在胸墙上爆炸。

conceited [kən'si:tɪd] *adj.* 自负的；骄傲自大的

例 Even if we achieve great success in our work, we should not be conceited.
即使我们在工作中取得了很大的成绩，也不应该自满。

语法知识点 Grammar Points

① I think it not improbable that I am still living just because I was able to write such a book.

这个句子中,"improbable"做"think"的宾语补足语,"it"是形式宾语,指代"that I am living..."同样用法的词和短语还有"consider"、"feel"、"find"等。

例 Reaching the age of 20, he found it impossible to live carefreely.
20岁的时候,他发现无忧无虑的生活是不可能的。

② I know of no one of them who entertains the ideas expressed in this book.

这个句子中"expressed in this book"做后置定语修饰"ideas",省略了"which/ that is"。定语从句中关系代词代替先行词做主语,且从句中有be动词时,关系代词和be动词均可省略。

例 The messages displayed in his speech are inspiring.
他的讲话中传递出来的信息很振奋人心。

③ I am conceited enough to think that I have not thought individually but collectively.

这个句子中运用"enough to do something"的结构表示"足够……做某事"。

例 She is not brave enough to climb the tree.
她不敢爬树。

经典名句 Famous Classics

1. Walking with a friend in the dark is better than walking alone in the light. — Helen Keller
在黑暗中与朋友并肩同行好过在光亮中独自行走。——海伦·凯勒

2. Friendship is always a sweet responsibility, never an opportunity. — Khalil Gibran
友谊是甜蜜的责任,而不是机遇。——纪伯伦

3. My best friend is the one who brings out the best in me. — Henry

Ford

最好的朋友促使我变成最好的自己。——福特

4. Prejudices are what fools use for reason. — Friedrich Nietzsche
  偏见是愚者思考的方式。——弗里德里希·尼采

5. Suspicion is the poison of friendship . — St, Augustine, Bishop of hippo
  怀疑是对友谊所下的毒药。——希波主教 圣奥古斯丁

6. A friend is a second self.
  朋友是第二个自我。

7. Friendship is like money, easier made than kept. — Samuel Butler
  友谊如金钱一般，容易得到却不易保持。——塞缪尔·巴特勒

8. Happiness is a perfume you cannot pour on others without getting a few drops on yourself. — Emerson
  幸福犹如香水，你不可能泼向别人而自己却不沾几滴。——爱默生

读书笔记

08 John Keats to Percy Bysshe Shelley
约翰·济慈致珀西·比希·雪莱

Hampstead, 16th August, 1820

My Dear Shelley,

I am very much gratified that you, in a foreign country, and with a mind almost over occupied, should write to me in the strain of the letter beside me. If I do not take advantage of your invitation it will be prevented by a circumstance I have very much at heart to prophesy—There is no doubt that an English winter would put an end to me, and do so in a lingering hateful manner, therefore I must either voyage or journey to Italy as a soldier marches up to a battery.

My nerves at present are the worst part of me, yet they feel **soothed** when I think that come what extreme may, I shall not be destined to remain in one spot long enough to take a hatred of any four particular **bed-posts**.

I am glad you take any pleasure in my poor poem which I would willingly take the trouble to unwrite, if possible, did I care so much as I have done about reputation. I received a copy of the *Cenci*, as from yourself, from Hunt.

我亲爱的雪莱：

你身处异乡，事务繁忙，竟然还能不辞辛劳地给我写信（它就在我旁边），这真是让我不胜感激。如果我不接受你的邀请，那么一种我早已预知的情形就会阻止我前往。毫无疑问，英国的冬天会让我的病情雪上加霜，甚至会慢慢地折磨我直到死去。因此我必须像战士奔赴战场一样前去意大利，无论走水路还是陆路。

现在我的神经是最糟糕的，然而我一想到，我无论病到何种地步，都不会向命运妥协，久卧病榻以至于对任何一张床感到厌恶，他们就稍稍缓和一点了。

拙作承蒙你的喜爱让我非常高兴，如果我还像过去那样在意名声的话，而且如果可能的话，我会很乐意将他们抹掉。我从亨特那里收到一份《珊奇》的复印本，和从你那里收到也是一样的。其中只有

There is only one part of it I am judge of—the poetry and dramatic effect—which by many spirits nowadays is considered the **Mammon**. A modern work it is said must have a purpose, which may be the God—an artist must serve Mammon—he must have "self-concentration"—selfishness perhaps. You, I am sure, will forgive me for sincerely remarking that you might curb your **magnanimity** and be more of an artist, and load every rift of your subject with **ore**. The thought of such discipline must fall like cold chains upon you, who perhaps never sat with your wings furled for six months together. And is this not extraordinary talk for the writer of *Endymion*, whose mind was like a pack of scattered cards? I am picked up and sorted to a **pip**.

My Imagination is a monastery and I am its monk. You must explain my **metaphysics** to yourself. I am in expectation of *Prometheus* every day. Could I have my own wish for its interest effected, you would have it still in manuscript, or be but now putting an end to the second act. I remember you advising me not to publish my first-**blights**, on Hampstead Heath—I am returning advice upon your hands. Most of the Poems in the volume I send you have been written above two years, and

一部分我能稍做评价——诗歌和戏剧效果，这一点被现在很多人视为财神。据说，现代作品必须有特定的目的，可能就是指这位神；艺术家必须供奉它；艺术家必须关注自我，也可能是自私。我相信你会原谅我的直言相劝，你应该少一点崇高的品质，多一点艺术家的风格，让字里行间的主题里都填满了金子。这样的约束就像将冰冷的镣铐强加于你，甚至你可能从来没有收起翅膀坐过半年吧。《恩底弥翁》的作者说这话很奇怪吧，过去他的思绪就像散落一地的纸牌般杂乱无章。现在我已经将它们捡起并重新理顺了。

如果我的想象是一座寺院，那么我就是居于其中的僧人。我这个玄学派的奇喻得你自己来解释。我每天都在期盼《普罗米修斯》。要是我的愿望灵验了的话，现在你应该还在继续创作吧——可能正在写第二幕的结尾了吧。我记得你劝我不要发表我早期关于汉普斯台德荒原的无病呻吟的诗，现在轮到我对你提出这一建议了。我寄给你的诗中大部分都是两年前写的，要不是为了增加收入，我本来不会把它们发表的。所以您可以看得出来，我现在足够愿意

would never have been published but from a hope of gain; so you see I am inclined enough to take your advice now.

I must express once more my deep sense of your kindness, adding my sincere thanks and respects for Mrs. Shelley. In the hope of soon seeing you I remain.

most sincerely yours
John Keats

接受你的意见了。

我必须再次感谢你的好意，并请转达我对雪莱夫人诚挚的感谢与敬意。

盼望着和您见面的那一刻！

永远是你最真挚的
约翰·济慈
1820年8月16日于汉普斯台德

单词解析 Word Analysis

soothe [suːð] *vt.* 安慰；缓和

例 It did not take long for the central bank to soothe investors' fears.
中央银行很快便消除了投资者的担忧。

bed-post ['bed,pəʊst] *n.* 床柱

例 His big slouch hat even was cocked jauntily over the bed-post.
他那边缘下垂的大帽子逍遥地歪戴在床柱子上。

Mammon ['mæmən] *n.* 财富，财神

例 She believes that our society teaches young people to worship Mammon.
她相信我们的社会教年轻人崇拜财神。

magnanimity [ˌmægnə'nɪmətɪ] *n.* 宽宏大量

例 The father of one victim spoke with remarkable magnanimity.
一名受害者的父亲以极为宽容的口吻发了言。

ore [ɔː(r)] *n.* 矿石；矿砂；矿

例 How many tons of ore can this machine crush in an hour?
这机器每小时可以破碎多少吨矿石？

pip [pɪp] *n.* （色子、骨牌、纸牌上的）点
例 There is a playing card marked with nine pips.
有标有9点的一张扑克牌。

metaphysics [ˌmetəˈfɪzɪks] *n.* 形而上学，玄学
例 Metaphysics is an accidental problem in the history of western philosophy.
形而上学在西方哲学史上是一个古老的问题。

blight [blaɪt] *n.* 破坏因素；祸根；阴影
例 Manchester still suffers from urban blight and unacceptable poverty.
曼彻斯特仍然受到城区脏乱和严重贫困问题的困扰。

语法知识点 Grammar Points

① **Therefore I must either voyage or journey to Italy as a soldier marches up to a battery.**

这个句子中"as"引导一个比较状语从句，意为"正如，像……一样"。
例 She is so eager to read the book as a hungry man is eager to get some bread.
她是如此想读这本书，就像饥饿的人想要得到面包一样。

② **I shall not be destined to remain in one spot long enough to take a hatred of any four particular bed-posts.**

这个句子中用到了提喻的修辞手法，用"bed-post"指代"bed"。常见的还有用"hand"指代"worker"等。
例 To finish the project, we need more hands.
要完成这个项目，我们需要更多的人手。

③ **I am glad you take any pleasure in my poor poem which I would willingly take the trouble to unwrite, if possible, did I care so much as I have done about reputation.**

这个句子中用到了一个插入语"if possible",意为"如果可能的话",这是"if"和"when"引导状语从句时的特殊用法,常见的搭配有"if/when + necessary/ possible/"。

例 If necessary, we will resort to military action.
如果有必要的话,我们会付诸军事行动。

经典名句 *Famous Classics*

1. Familiar paths and old friends are the best.
   熟路好遵循,老友最可珍。

2. Books, like friends, should be few and well chosen.
   书籍如朋友,应该少而精。

3. Although the world is full of suffering, it is full also of the overcoming of it. — Hellen Keller
   虽然世界多苦难,但苦难总是能战胜的。——海伦·凯勒

4. Coward die many times before their death. — William Shakespeare
   懦夫在死之前就已经死过很多次了。——威廉·莎士比亚

5. A great poem is a fountain forever overflowing with the waters of wisdom and delight. — Shelley
   一首伟大的诗犹如一座喷泉,不断地喷出智慧和快乐的泉水。——雪莱

6. Friendship is love without his wings.
   友谊是不带翅膀的爱情。

7. A thing of beauty is a joy forever: its loveliness increases; it will never pass into nothingness. — John Keats
   美的事物是永恒的喜悦:其可爱日增;永远不会消失。——约翰·济慈

09 Ralph Waldo Emerson to Walt Whitman
拉尔夫·瓦尔多·爱默生致沃尔特·惠特曼

Concord, Mass., July 21, 1885

Dear Sir,

I am not **blind to** the worth of the wonderful gift of *Leaves of Grass*. I find it the most extraordinary piece of wit and wisdom that America has yet contributed. I am very happy in reading it, as great power makes us happy. It meets the demand I am always making of what seems the **sterile** and **stingy** Nature, as if too much handiwork or too much **lymph** in the temperament were making our western wits fat and mean. I give you joy of your free and brave thought. I have great joy in it. I find incomparable things said incomparably well, as they must be. I find the courage of treatment, which so delights us, and which large perception only can inspire.

I greet you at the beginning of a great career, which must yet have had a long foreground somewhere, for such a start. I rubbed my eyes a little to see if this sunbeam were no illusion; but the solid sense of the book is a sober certainty. It has the best merits, namely,

亲爱的先生：

《草叶集》如同天赐，无比珍贵，我无法将之忽视。我认为，这是美国历史上最具才华与智慧的作品了。这书读起来十分愉快，因为其中表达的强大的力量让人快乐。《草叶集》满足了我向似乎有些贫瘠和匮乏的大自然所能要求的一切，就好像太多的人工修饰或太过迂腐懒惰正把我们西方的才子都变得既肥胖又刻薄。你有自由大胆的思想应该快乐才是呀，我就因此十分高兴。我发现你把无可比拟的事物用无可比拟的方式表达了出来，正像他们应该的那样。我发现这种大胆的处理方法让我们如此愉快，也只有知识渊博的人才能做到。

我要祝贺你步入这个伟大的职业，有如此好的开端，你一定会走得更远。我揉了揉眼睛以确定这阳光是不是幻觉。但是书在掌中的厚重感是确切无

of **fortifying** and encouraging.

I did not know until, I, last night, saw the book advertised in a newspaper, that I could trust the name as real and available for a post-office.

I wish to see my **benefactor**, and have felt much like striking my tasks, and visiting New York to pay you my respects.

R. W. Emerson

疑的。这本书最大的优点在于它能够给人力量、鼓舞人心。

直到昨晚在报纸上看到《草叶集》的广告，我才确认作者的名字是真实的、可以通信的。

你给我带来了如此大的喜悦，所以我盼望着能与你见面。我甚至想要撇下手头的工作，去纽约拜访你。

R. W. 爱默生
1855年7月21日
于马萨诸塞州康科德

单词解析 Word Analysis

be blind to something 对……视而不见

例 We should not be blind to global warming, which is one of the biggest environment problems nowadays.
我们不应该对全球变暖视而不见，它是当今最大的环境问题之一。

sterile ['steraɪl] *adj.* 无菌的；贫瘠的

例 Too much time has been wasted in sterile debate.
在毫无新意的辩论上已经浪费了太多时间。

stingy ['stɪndʒi] *adj.* 小气的，吝啬的

例 she is extremely frugal, not to say stingy.
不说她吝啬，至少她也是极其节俭的。

lymph [lɪmf] *n.* 淋巴

例 She has got an inflammation of lymph.
她的淋巴发炎了。

fortify ['fɔːtɪfaɪ] *vt.* （在物质或精神上）加强，增强

例 The volunteers were fortified by their patriotic belief.
爱国信念更加坚定了志愿者们的信心。

benefactor ['benɪfæktə(r)] *n.* 恩人，捐助者

例 An anonymous benefactor stepped in to provide the prize money.
一个匿名捐助者施以援手提供了奖金。

语法知识点 *Grammar Points*

① **I am very happy in reading it, as great power makes us happy.**

这个句子中"as"引导原因状语从句，意为"因为……"。

例 As there is no support from his family, Kevin needs to rely on himself.
因为没有家里的帮助，凯文必须依靠自己。

② **I did not know until, I, last night, saw the book advertised in a newspaper, that I could trust the name as real and available for a post-office.**

这个句子中用到了"not... until..."结构，表示"直到……才……"。

例 He did not know it was me until I took off my sunglasses.
直到我取下墨镜，他才认出我。

经典名句 *Famous Classics*

1. A life without a friend is a life without a sun.
   人生没有了朋友就犹如失去了阳光。

2. Don't try to win a friend by presenting gifts. You should instead contribute your sincere love and learn how to win others' heart through appropriate ways. — Socrates
   不要用馈赠去获得朋友，你必须奉献你诚挚的爱，学会怎样用适当的方法来赢得别人的心。——古希腊哲学家 苏格拉底

3. Friends are sunshine in life. — Ibsen
   朋友是生活中的阳光。——易卜生

4. A bosom friend afar brings distant land near.
   海内存知己，天涯若比邻。

5. You think I'm the son of fate; in fact, I'm creating my own destiny. — Emerson
你们认为我是命运之子,实际上,我却在创造着我自己的命运。——爱默生

6. If two people read the same book, they have a bond between them.
如果两个人读过同一本书,他们之间就有了一条纽带。

7. Flaming enthusiasm, backed up by horse sense and persistence, is the quality that most frequently makes for success. — Dale Carnegie
永不熄灭的热情加以常识和坚持不懈是成功的重要素质。——戴尔·卡耐基

8. The talent for being happy is appreciating and liking what you have, instead of what you don't have. — Woody Allen
欣赏和喜欢你拥有的东西,而不是你没有的东西,你才能快乐。——伍迪·艾伦

读书笔记

10 Benjamin Disraeli to Thomas Carlyle
本杰明·迪斯雷利致托马斯·卡莱尔

Bournemouth, 27 Dec. 1874

Sir,

A government should recognize intellect. It **elevates** and sustains the tone of a nation. But it is an office which, adequately to fulfill, requires both courage and **discrimination**, as there is a chance of falling into **favouritism** and patronizing **mediocrity**, which, instead of elevating the national feeling, would eventually degrade or debase it.

In recommending Her Majesty to **fit out** an Arctic expedition, and in suggesting other measures of that class, her Government have shown their sympathy with science. I wish that the position of high letters should be equally acknowledged; but this is not so easy, because it is in the necessity of things that the test of merit cannot be so precise in literature as in science.

When I consider the literary world, I can see only two living names which, I would **fain** believe, will be remembered; and they stand out in uncontested superiority. One is that of a poet; if not

先生：

一个政府应该尊重人才。这样能提高和维持国家的文化格调。但是要充分履行这一职责需要勇气和甄别力。因为很有可能出现任人唯亲和重用庸人的情况，而这不仅不会提升民族情感，反而会最终腐化、破坏民族情感。

政府向女王陛下建议组建北极探险队，以及其他有关事宜时，显示了对科学的热爱。我希望高雅文学也能受到同样的对待。但这不是那么容易，因为文学作品的成就不可能和科学一样受到精准的评价。

要说起文学界来，我看只有两个人的名字能永垂不朽，这我倒乐得相信。这两人十分出色，有着毫无疑义的优越性。一个是一位诗人，一位就算不是伟大的也是真正的诗人；另一个就是你自己。

我已经建议女王陛下授予丁尼生从男爵爵位，如果你想

a great poet, a real one; and the other is your own.

I have advised the Queen to offer to conquer a **baronetcy** on Mr. Tennyson, and the same distinction should be at your command, if you like it. But I have remembered that, like myself, you are childless, and may not care for hereditary honours. I have therefore made up my mind, if agreeable to yourself, to recommend to Her Majesty to confer on you the highest distinction for merit at her command, and which, I believe, has never yet been conferred by her except for direct services to the State. And that is the Grand Cross of the Bath.

I will speak with frankness on another point. It is not well that, in the sunset of your life, you should be disturbed by common cares. I see no reason why a great author should not receive from the nation a pension as well as a lawyer and a statesman. Unfortunately the personal power of Her Majesty in this respect is limited; but still it is in the Queen's capacity to settle on an individual an amount equal to a good **fellowship**, and which was cheerfully accepted and enjoyed by the great spirit of Johnson, and the pure integrity of Southey.

Have the goodness to let me know

要，你也可以获得这一荣誉。但是我记得，和我一样，你没有子女，可能并不在意世袭的荣誉。因此，我决定，如果你也赞同的话，建议女王陛下将她所能授予的最高荣誉勋章授予你。除了对国家有直接贡献的人，这一勋章是不予颁发的。它就是巴斯大十字勋章。

我还有一点要坦白说明。人到了暮年的时候还为俗事烦忧，是有损健康的。我不明白一个伟大的作家为什么不能和律师以及政治家一样获得国家的津贴。遗憾的是，女王陛下在这件事情上力量有限；但是陛下仍然有能力奖给个人一笔丰厚的研究资金，伟大的塞缪尔·约翰逊和正直的罗伯特·骚塞就曾欣然接受过这笔奖金。

不知你的想法如何？还望告知。

先生，荣幸作为
你忠实的仆人
本杰明·迪斯雷利
1874年12月27日于伯恩茅斯

your feelings on these subjects.
>
> **I have the honour to remain, Sir,**
> **Your faithful servant,**
> **B. Disraeli**

单词解析 *Word Analysis*

elevate ['elɪveɪt] *vt.* 提高；增加

例 Democracy might elevate the common man to a position of political superiority.
民主也许能提升普通人的政治地位，让他们产生优越感。

discrimination [dɪˌskrɪmɪ'neɪʃn] *n.* 区别对待；歧视

例 Discrimination by employers on the grounds of race and nationality was illegal.
雇主以种族和国籍为由歧视员工是非法的。

favoritism ['feɪvərɪtɪzəm] *n.* 偏爱，偏袒，任人唯亲

例 We tried to meet both children's needs without the appearance of favoritism or unfairness.
我们尽力对两个孩子的需要都予以满足，而不显得有所偏向或袒护。

mediocrity [ˌmiːdi'ɒkrəti] *n.* 庸人，平庸，平凡

例 Surrounded by mediocrities, he can seem a towering intellectual.
在周围一群泛泛之辈的衬托之下，他就像一个鹤立鸡群的智者。

fit out 以……装备，供给……以必需品

例 Father has bought enough food to fit out a whole family.
爸爸买了充足的食物，足够全家人用的。

fain [feɪn] *adv.* 欣然，乐意地

例 He would fain stay at home.
他真乐意待在家里。

baronetcy ['bærənətsi] *n.* 从男爵爵位

例 Sir Arthur was the holder of a baronetcy dating back to Charles I.
阿瑟爵士拥有的从男爵爵位可追溯至查理一世时代。

fellowship ['feləʊʃɪp] 友谊；团体；研究资金，研究生奖学金

例 A research fellowship came up at Girton and I applied for it and got it.
格顿学院设立了一项研究奖学金，我提出申请并且成功获得。

语法知识点 Grammar Points

① **I wish that the position of high letters should be equally acknowledged.**

这个句子中使用了虚拟语气，"wish"其后的宾语从句中可用"would/could/might/should + 动词原形"表达对将来发生的事情的愿望。

例 Teddy wishes that there would be endless cakes to eat.
泰迪希望有吃不完的蛋糕。

② **But this is not so easy, because it is in the necessity of things that the test of merit cannot be so precise in literature as in science.**

这个句子中"not so... as..."为同级比较结构的否定形式，意为"……不如……"。

例 His job requires not so much professional knowledge as mine.
他的工作要求的专业知识不如我的多。

经典名句 Famous Classics

1. Adventure is the vitaminizing element in histories both individual and social. — William Bolitho
   冒险对个人历史和社会历史都是具有生气的东西。——威廉·博里索

2. Nothing venture, nothing have. — John Heywood
   不入虎穴，焉得虎子。——约翰·海伍德

3. Youth live on hope, old age on remembrance. — French Proverb
   年轻人生活在希望之中，老年人却生活在回忆里。——法国谚语

4. A nation reveals itself not only by the men it produces, but also by the men it honours, the men it remembers. — John F. Kennedy
   一个民族不仅通过它所造就的人，也通过它给予荣誉的人和铭记的人展示自己。——肯尼迪

5. We have no permanent friend, We have no permanent enemies, We just have permanent interests. — Benjamin Disraeli
   没有永恒的朋友，没有永恒的敌人，只有永恒的利益。——本杰明·迪斯雷利

6. Cease to struggle and you cease to live. — Thomas Carlyle
   生命不息，奋斗不止！——托马斯·卡莱尔

7. Personality is to a man what perfume is to a flower. — Charles Schwabe
   品格之于人犹如香味之于花。——查理·施瓦布

8. Wealth is the test of a man's character.
   财富是对一个人品格的试金石。

读书笔记

11 Abraham Lincoln to John D. Johnson
亚伯拉罕·林肯致约翰·约翰斯顿

December 24, 1848

Dear Johnson,

　　Your request for eighty dollars, I do not think it best to **comply** now. At the various times when I have helped you a little, you have said to me, "We can get along very well now," but in a very short time I find you in the same difficulty again. Now this can only happen by some **defect** in your conduct. What the defect is, I think I know. You are not lazy, and still you are an idler. I doubt whether since I saw you, you have done a good whole day's work, in any one day. You do not very much dislike to work, and still you do not work much, merely because it does not seem to you that you could get much for it.

　　This habit of uselessly wasting time, is the whole difficulty; it is **vastly** important to you, and still more so to your children, that you should break this habit. It is more important to them, because they have longer to live, and can keep out of an idle habit before they are in it, easier than they can get out

亲爱的约翰斯顿：

　　至于你要求的80美元，我想，现在就答应你不是最好的办法。每当我给你一点帮助，你就对我说："我们现在可以过得很好了。"但是很快，我发现你又处于同样的困境中了。那么这只能是由于你的品行上出了差错。我想我知道是什么差错。你不算懒惰，却游手好闲。我怀疑，自从见到你以来，你是否好好地工作过一整天，哪怕一天也好。你并不十分讨厌工作，但你却不怎么干活，原因是对你而言，从工作中能得到的似乎并不多。

　　这种空耗时间的习惯就是症结所在。改掉这种习惯，对你很重要，对你的孩子们更重要。对孩子们更重要是因为他们要活的时间更长，可以在染上无所事事的毛病之前就把它戒除掉，这比染上之后再戒容易多了。

　　现在你需要一笔现成的

after they are in.

You are now in need of some ready money; and what I **propose** is, that you shall go to work, "**tooth and nail**," for somebody who will give you money for it.

Let father and your boys take charge of your things at home—prepare for a crop, and make the crop, and you go to work for the best money wages, or in **discharge** of any debt you owe, that you can get. And to secure you a fair reward for your labor, I now promise you that for every dollar you will, between this and the first of May, get for your own labor either in money or in your own **indebtedness**, I will then give you one other dollar.

By this, if you hire yourself at ten dollars a month, from me you will get ten more, making twenty dollars a month for your work. In this, I do not mean you shall go off to St. Louis, or the lead mines, or the gold mines, in California, but I mean for you to go at it for the best wages you can get close to home—in Coles County.

Now if you do this, you will soon be out of debt, and what is better, you will have a habit that will keep you from getting in debt again. But if I should now clear you out, next year you will be just as deep in as ever. You say you would almost give your place in Heaven for $70 or $80. Then you value

钱，我给你的建议是，去工作，拼命赚钱。

把家里的事交给父亲和孩子们——耕种劳作。而你找一份你所能找得到的有最丰厚薪资的工作，或是能偿还清你所欠下的所有债务的工作。为了保证你的辛勤劳动能有公正的回报，我现在承诺你，从今天起到5月1日为止，你工作挣得的每一块钱或还清的每一块钱的债务，我将再额外给你一美元。

这样算来，你每月的工资是10美元的话，从我这里将再得到10美元，相当于你每月凭劳动可以挣得20美元。我并不是让你去圣路易斯或者加利福尼亚的铅矿、金矿工作，而是在离家不远的找你所能得到的最优厚待遇的工作——就在柯尔斯小镇。

现在如果你这样做的话，你很快就会摆脱债务了，更好的是，你会养成一个让你不再欠债的好习惯。但我要是现在替你还清债务，明年你又会和以前一样背上一大笔债。你说你几乎愿意放弃你在天堂的席位，就为了70或80美元。那你把你在天堂的席位想得太廉价了，因为我能保证，照我说的做，你四五个月的工资就够七八十美元了。你说如果我

your place in Heaven very cheaply, for I am sure you can with the offer I make you get the seventy or eighty dollars for four or five month's work. You say if I furnish you the money you will **deed** me the land, and if you don't pay the money back, you will deliver possession—

Nonsense! If you can't now live with the land, how will you then live without it? You have always been kind to me, and I do not now mean to be unkind to you. On the contrary, if you but follow my advice, you will find it worth more than eight times eighty dollars to you.

Affectionately,
Your brother
A.Lincoln

借钱给你，你就把田地转让给我；如果你没有还钱，就把财产给我——

简直是胡话！你现在有田地都不能生活，没了田地又该怎么活下去呢？你对我一向很好，我也不想对你刻薄。相反，如果你采纳我的建议，你会发现这比80美元更值钱。

关心你的
哥哥
亚·林肯

单词解析 Word Analysis

comply [kəmˈplaɪ] *v.* 遵从；服从；顺从

例 The commander said that the army would comply with the ceasefire.
指挥官说军队会遵守停火协议。

defect [ˈdiːfekt] *n.* 瑕疵，毛病

例 A report has pointed out the defects of the present system.
一份报告指出了当前体制存在的毛病。

vastly [ˈvɑːstli] *adv.* 极大地，广大地

例 Like most of my contemporaries, I grew up in a vastly different world.
和大多数同辈人一样，我生长在一个截然不同的世界。

propose [prəˈpəʊz] *vt.* 提议；建议

例 It was George who first proposed that we dry clothes in that locker.
是乔治首先提议我们把衣服挂在那个储物柜里晾干的。

tooth and nail 拼命

例 He fought tooth and nail to keep his job.
他竭尽全力保住自己的工作。

discharge [dɪs'tʃɑːdʒ] *vt.* 清偿（债务）

例 The goods will be sold for a fraction of their value in order to discharge the debt.
货物将被贱价卖出以清偿债务。

indebtedness [ɪn'detɪdnəs] *n.* 受恩惠；亏欠；债务

例 A sense of gratitude and indebtedness to others is an important wellspring of a generous and virtuous life.
懂得感恩和对他人的负债感是慷慨和善良生活的重要源泉。

deed [diːd] *vt.* 立契转让

例 He decided to deed the ownership of houses over to his youngest son.
他决定立契把房子所有权转让给最小的儿子。

语法知识点 *Grammar Points*

① **By this, if you hire yourself at ten dollars a month, from me you will get ten more, making twenty dollars a month for your work.**

这个句子中"if"引导条件状语从句，从句中用了一般现在时，主句中是一般将来时，表示事情发生的概率很高。

例 If you go and ask him, he will tell you the answer you want.
如果你去问他，他会告诉你你想要的答案。

② **If you will but follow my advice, you will find it worth more than eight times eighty dollars to you.**

这个句子中"but"不表示转折，相当于"just""only"，是副词，意为"只，仅仅"。

例 This is but a small failure, and we sure can get over it.
这只是一个小小的失败，我们一定可以熬过去的。

经典名句 Famous Classics

1. I believe in work, hard work, and long hours of work. Men do not breakdown from overwork, but from worry and dissipation. — Charles Evans Hughes
我相信工作、努力工作及长时间的工作；过度工作不会让人崩溃，但忧虑及放纵自己却会让人崩溃。——查尔斯·埃文斯·休斯

2. It proves, on close examination, that work is less boring than amusing oneself. — Charles Baudelaire
仔细研究后，你会发现，工作不会比自我消遣还无聊。——查理士·波特莱尔

3. The power of work, and the power of creativity, can be your salvation. — Nicole Kidman
工作的力量、创新的力量，可以成为你的救赎。——妮可·基德曼

4. Pleasure in the job puts perfection in the work. — Aristotle
乐在工作才有完美表现。——亚里士多德

5. You build your future. It isn't handed to you. — *House of Cards*
未来靠自己努力，而非靠人施予。——《纸牌屋》

6. Progress is the activity of today and the assurance of tomorrow. — Emerson
进步是今天的活动，明天的保证。——爱默生

7. Lazy is a mother, she has a son: robbery, and a daughter: hunger. — Hugo
懒散是一个母亲，她有一个儿子——抢劫，还有一个女儿——饥饿。——雨果

8. Never turn down a job because you think it's too small. You don't know where it can lead. — Julia Morgan
绝不要因为一个工作微不足道而拒绝它，你不知道它可以引领你去哪里。——茱丽亚·摩根

12 Abraham Lincoln to Mrs. Lydia Bixby
亚伯拉罕·林肯致莉迪亚·毕克斯比夫人

Executive Mansion, Washington, November 21, 1864

Dear Madam,

I have been shown in the files of the War Department a statement of the Adjutant General of Massachusetts that you are the mother of five sons who have died gloriously on the field of battle. I feel how weak and fruitless must be any word of mine which should attempt to **beguile** you from the grief of a loss so overwhelming. But I cannot refrain from tendering you the consolation that may be found in the thanks of the Republic they dies to save. I pray that our Heavenly Father may **assuage** the anguish of your bereavement, and leave you only the cherished memory of the loved and lost, and the **solemn** pride that must be yours to have laid so costly a sacrifice upon the altar of freedom.

Yours, very sincerely and respectfully,
　　　　　　　　　　　A.Lincoln

亲爱的夫人：

在陆军部递呈的文件中，有一份马萨诸塞军区副官长的报告说你的五个儿子都在战场上光荣牺牲。我感到我的任何话语都十分苍白无力，不能让你从如此巨大的丧子之痛中解脱出来。但是我还是忍不住代表共和国对这五位为国捐躯的战士表示感谢，希望能给你带去一丝安慰。我向天父祈祷，希望他能纾缓你的丧子之痛，只把对逝去爱子的美好回忆留在你的心中。你在自由神坛上的献祭如此代价惨重，这种庄严的自豪感必须属于你。

顺致真诚的敬意
亚伯拉罕·林肯
1864年11月21日
于华盛顿总统府

单词解析 Word Analysis

Executive Mansion 白宫，行政官邸

例 The White House used to have other names like the Executive Mansion and the President's House.
白宫过去还有其他名字，比如，行政官邸和总统府。

beguile [bɪ'gaɪl] *vt.* 吸引

例 His paintings beguiled the Prince of Wales.
他的画把威尔士亲王给迷住了。

assuage [ə'sweɪdʒ] *vt.* 缓和，减轻

例 To assuage his wife's grief, he took her on a tour of Europe.
为了减轻妻子的悲痛，他带她去了欧洲旅游。

solemn ['sɒləm] *adj.* 严肃的，庄严的

例 His behaviour was not in keeping with the solemn occasion.
他的举止与这庄严的场合不协调。

语法知识点 Grammar Points

① **I feel how weak and fruitless must be any word of mine which should attempt to beguile you from the grief of a loss so overwhelming.**

这个句子中"how"引导一个宾语从句，而宾语从句由"how"引导时，其后必须紧跟形容词或副词。

例 It's hard for him to imagine how much money this company can make a year.
他很难想象这家公司一年能挣多少钱。

② **I pray that our Heavenly Father may assuage the anguish of your bereavement, and leave you only the cherished memory of the loved and lost.**

这个句子中"the loved and lost"表示"爱着的并且失去了的人"。"the + adj."可以用来表示一类人。

例 The aristocratic has a set of strict rules of behavior.
贵族有严格的行为规范。

经典名句 Famous Classics

1. One of the best soldiers who should have the best ending in the final battle was the last bullet hit, in the last breath to see the victory of the flag before rising. — General Patton
   一个最好的战士应有的最好的结局就是在最后的战斗中被最后一颗子弹击中,在咽下最后一口气之前看到胜利的旗帜升起。——巴顿将军

2. In peace the sons bury their fathers, but in war the fathers bury their sons. — Croesus
   在和平年代中,儿子埋葬父亲。但是在战争中,父亲埋葬儿子。——克洛苏斯

3. Come home with this shield or upon it.
   回来的时候要么带着你的盾牌要么躺在上面。

4. We make war that we may live in peace. — Aristotle
   战争是为了和平。——亚里士多德

5. How could anyone ever know of the price paid by soldiers in terror, agony and bloodshed, if they'd never been to places like Normandy, Bastogne, or Haguenau? — *Band of Brothers*
   人们怎么能了解士兵们在惊恐、痛苦与血泊中的牺牲,如果他们从未置身于像诺曼底、巴斯通,或是哈根努那样的地方?——《兄弟连》

6. Only when one plunges into the powerful current of the times will one's life shine brilliantly. — Abraham Lincoln
   一个人只有投身于伟大的时代洪流中,他的生命才会闪耀出光彩。——亚伯拉罕·林肯

7. There is nothing that war has ever achieved we could not better achieve without it. — Havelock Ellis
   没有一件我们靠战争完成的事,不能以更好的方式完成。——哈维洛克·艾利斯

8. Affliction comes to us, not to make us sad but sober; not to make us sorry but wise. — H.G. Wells
痛苦的降临，是要让我们清醒不是难过，让我们更有智慧而不是懊悔。——赫伯特·乔治·威尔斯

读书笔记

13 Charles Darwin to R. W. Darwin
查尔斯·达尔文致罗伯特·达尔文

Maer, 31 August 1831

My Dear Father,

I am afraid I am going to make you again very uncomfortable. But, upon consideration, I think you will excuse me once again, stating my opinions on the offer of the voyage. My excuse and reason is the different way all the Wedgwoods view the subject from what you and my sisters do.

I have given Uncle Jos what I **fervently** trust is an accurate and full list of your objections, and he is kind enough to give his opinions on all. The list and his answers will be enclosed. But may I get of you one favour, it will be doing me the greatest kindness, if you send me a decided answer, yes or no? If the latter, I should be most ungrateful if I did not **implicitly yield** to your better judgment, and to the kindest indulgence you have shown me all through my life; and you may rely upon it I will never mention the subject again. If your answer should be yes, I

我亲爱的父亲：

我恐怕又要让您感到不安了。但是，再三考虑后，我想我还是要陈述一下我对这次出航机会的想法，请您原谅。这是因为韦奇伍德（乔赛亚·韦奇伍德，达尔文舅舅及后来的岳父，译注）一家在这件事情上和您以及姐妹们的看法不同。

我给乔赛亚舅舅列举了您的反对原因，我十分相信这就是您的准确的全部理由了。他十分友好地逐条给出了意见。我会附上您反对原因的清单以及舅舅的回答。但是如果我能得到您的一个帮助，我将不胜感激——您能给我一个决定性的回答，行还是不行吗？如果是不行，那我就绝对服从您更精明的判断，报答您从小到大对我的仁慈与照顾，否则我就太不孝了；我也绝不会再提起这件事。如果是行，我就会直

will go directly to Henslow and consult **deliberately** with him, and then come to Shrewsbury.

The danger appears to me and all the Wedgwoods not great. The expense can not be serious, and the time I do not think, anyhow, would be more thrown away than if I stayed at home. But pray do not consider that I am so **bent on** going that. I would for one single moment hesitate, if you thought that after a short period you should continue uncomfortable.

I must again state I cannot think it would unfit me **hereafter** for a steady life. I do hope this letter will not give you much uneasiness. I will send it by the car tomorrow morning; if you make up your mind directly will you send me an answer on the following day by the same means? If this letter should not find you at home, I hope you will answer as soon as you conveniently can.

I do not know what to say about Uncle Jos' kindness; I can never forget how he interests himself about me.

Believe me, my dear father,
Your affectionate son,
Charles Darwin

接去找亨斯洛，和他好好商量一下，然后前往什鲁斯伯里。

我和韦奇伍德一家都觉得危险不是那么大。花费不可能很多，而且所需的时间，我想，不会比我在家里挥霍的时间还要多。但是我祈祷您不要以为我铁了心要去远航，如果您过了一段时间还会觉得不愉快、不安的话，我会毫不犹豫地放弃这一想法的。

我必须重申，这次出航不会让我对以后的安稳生活感到不适应。我真的希望这封信不会让您感到那么不安。明早我会把信交给马车带去给您。如果您可以直接做好决定，您能在次日也用同样的方式回信给我吗？如果信寄到时，您不在家的话，我希望在您方便之时尽快回信。

我不知道该怎么描述乔赛亚舅舅的好意，我永远不能忘记他对我有多么关心。

相信我，亲爱的父亲
爱你的儿子
查尔斯·达尔文
1831年8月31日于麦尔

单词解析 Word Analysis

fervently ['fɜːvəntlɪ] *adv.* 热烈地，热情地，强烈地

例 I fervently hope he recognizes and understands the burden that's on his shoulders.
我热诚地希望他能认识到并懂得自己肩负的重任。

implicitly [ɪmˈplɪsɪtlɪ] *adv.* 无疑问地；无保留地

例 We trust each other implicitly and I think it's been of benefit to our company.
我们互相信任，我想我们公司也从中受益。

yield [jiːld] *vt.* 屈服，投降

例 Boston's traditional drab brick was slow to yield to the modern glass palaces in so many American urban areas.
波士顿传统而单调的砖石建筑并没有迅速被许多美国城市地区流行的现代玻璃大厦所取代。

deliberately [dɪˈlɪbərətli] *adv.* 深思熟虑地；从容不迫地

例 The prime minister acted calmly and deliberately.
总理表现得冷静而审慎。

bent on doing something 决心做某事

例 They are always bent on interfering in other countries' internal affairs.
他们总是蓄意干涉别国内政。

hereafter [ˌhɪərˈɑːftə(r)] *adv.* 今后，从此以后

例 I realised how hard life was going to be for me hereafter.
我意识到从今以后我的生活将会多么艰难。

语法知识点 Grammar Points

① But, upon consideration, I think you will excuse me once again, stating my opinions on the offer of the voyage.

这个句子中"upon consideration"意为"基于考虑","upon"和"on"都可接名词表示原因。

例 On your advice, I have made up my mind to go abroad.
因为听了您的建议,我决定出国。

② **But pray do not consider that I am so bent on going that I would for one single moment hesitate, if you thought that after a short period you should continue uncomfortable.**

这个句子中"so... that..."表示"如此……以至于……","that"引导结果状语从句,"so"后紧跟形容词或副词。

例 Her dinner was so well prepared that we wanted to be invited by her again.
她的晚餐准备得如此丰盛以至于我们想再被她邀请一次。

经典名句 Famous Classics

1. In the end, it's not the years in your life that count. It's the life in your years. — Abraham Lincoln
最终,重要的不是你人生里有多少岁数,而是你的岁数里有多少人生。——林肯

2. It is impossible to win the great prizes in life without running risks. — Theodore Roosevelt
不冒风险就不可能获得人生里的奖品。——西奥多·罗斯福

3. If you really want something, you have to be prepared to work very hard, take advantage of opportunity, and above all never give up. — Jane Goodall
若你真的很想做一件事,你得准备好非常努力、善用机会,而最重要的是绝不放弃。——珍妮·古道尔

4. As a well spent day brings happy sleep, so life well used brings happy death. — Leonardo da Vinci
好好利用白天可让人欣慰地入睡,好好利用人生可让人欣慰地离世。——达·芬奇

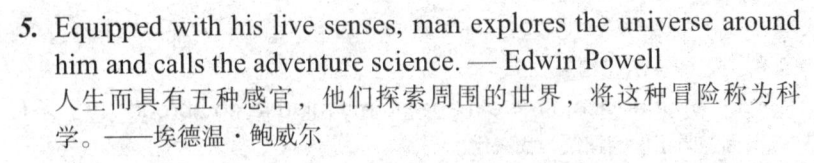

5. Equipped with his live senses, man explores the universe around him and calls the adventure science. — Edwin Powell
   人生而具有五种感官,他们探索周围的世界,将这种冒险称为科学。——埃德温·鲍威尔

6. Small opportunities are often the beginning of great enterprises. — Demosthenes
   微小的机会常常是伟大事业的开端。——德摩斯梯尼

7. A good opportunity is seldom presented, and is easily lost. — Publilius Syrus
   良机不常出现,而且容易错过。——帕布里利斯·希若思

8. Make hay while the sun shines. — English Proverb
   晒草要趁阳光好。——英国谚语

读书笔记

14 Henry David Thoreau to Ralph Waldo Emerson
亨利·大卫·梭罗致拉尔夫·瓦尔多·爱默生

February 12, 1843

Dear Friend,

As the packet still **tarries**, I will send you some thoughts, which I have lately relearned, as the latest public and private news.

How mean are our relations to one another! Let us pause till they are nobler. A little silence, a little rest, is good. It would be sufficient employment only to cultivate true ones.

The richest gifts we can bestow are the least marketable. We hate the kindness which we understand. A noble person confers no such gift as his whole confidence: none so exalts the giver and the receiver; it produces the truest gratitude. Perhaps it is only essential to friendship that some vital trust should have been reposed by the one in the other. I feel addressed and probed even to the remote parts of my being when one nobly shows, even in **trivial** things, an implicit faith in me. When such divine commodities are so near and cheap, how strange it should have

亲爱的朋友：

在包裹仍未寄出时，我想写下一些重新思考过的想法寄给你，就当作是最新的公共和私人新闻吧。

我们的关系是多么不堪啊！让我们冷静一下，让关系稍稍变得高尚一些吧。些许的沉默和片刻的休息是有利的。这样做，对培育真正的交情来说，已经足够了。

我们可以赠送的最昂贵的礼物恰恰是最不受人待见的。我们厌恶自己能够理解的善意。一个品格高尚的人最好的礼物莫过于他的全部信任——没有什么比这更能使送礼者和收礼者感到荣光；全部的信任会带来真心的感激。可能只有对友谊而言，一个人对另一个人的绝对信任才是至关重要的。当一个人对我展现出绝对的信任时，哪怕是在微不足道的事情上，我都会感到全身上下都受到了他的关注和探寻。这样神圣的商品离我们如

to be each day's discovery! A threat or a curse may be forgotten, but this mild trust translates me. I am no more of this earth; it acts **dynamically**; it changes my very substance. I cannot do what before I did. I cannot be what before I was. Other chains may be broken, but in the darkest night, in the remotest place, I trail this thread. Then things cannot happen. What if God were to confide in us for a moment! Should we not then be gods?

How subtle a thing is this confidence! Nothing sensible passes between; never any consequences are to be apprehended should it be misplaced. Yet something has **transpired**. A new behavior springs; the ship carries new ballast in her hold. A sufficiently great and generous trust could never be abused. It should be cause to lay down one's life, —which would not be to lose it. Can there be any mistake up there? Don't the gods know where to invest their wealth? Such confidence, too, would be reciprocal. When one **confides** greatly in you, he will feel the roots of an equal trust fastening themselves in him. When such trust has been received or reposed, we dare not speak, hardly see each other; our voices sound harsh and untrustworthy. We are as instruments which the Powers have dealt with. Through what **straits** would we not carry this little burden of a magnanimous

此的近、价格又如此的低，我们却要每天去寻找它，这多么奇怪啊！我不会记住威胁和诅咒，却会因这温和的信任而改变。我不再是凡人一个，这力量剧烈地作用在我身上，使我脱胎换骨。我不能像以前一样做事，也不能像以前一样做人。其他的链条可能会断裂，但在漆黑的夜里，在最遥远的地方，我循着"信任"这条线往前走。那么万事万物就会安然无恙了。要是上帝能信任我们、对我们托付机密就好了！那样我们难道不就和神一样了吗？

这信任是多么微妙啊！很少有人能感知到它，如果给错了人，也不会有什么影响。但某些事情其实已经发生了变化。一种新的行为产生了，船上也装载了新的压舱物。这样伟大至极、慷慨至极的信任是永远不会被滥用的。有人愿意为此付出生命，也不愿意失去它。难道是上帝犯了什么错误？神们难道都不知道该把财富投资在哪里吗？这样的信任也是相互的。一个人向你将秘密全盘托出时，他会深深地感受到你对他也有同样的信任。当我们接受或施予这样的信任时，我们是不敢说话的，甚至不敢看着对方；我们的声音听起来也很刺耳，好像不那么可靠。我们就

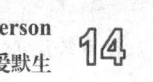

Henry David Thoreau to Ralph Waldo Emerson
亨利·大卫·梭罗致拉尔夫·瓦尔多·爱默生

trust! Yet no harm could possibly come, but simply faithlessness. Not a feather, not a straw, is **intrusted**; that packet is empty. It is only committed to us, and, as it were, all things are committed to us.

The kindness I have longest remembered has been of this sort, --the sort unsaid; so far behind the speaker's lips that almost it already lay in my heart. It did not have far to go to be communicated. The gods cannot misunderstand, man cannot explain. We communicate like the **burrows** of foxes, in silence and darkness, under ground. We are undermined by faith and love. How much more full is Nature where we think the empty space is than where we place the solids!—full of fluid influences. Should we ever communicate but by these? The spirit abhors a vacuum more than Nature. There is a tide which pierces the pores of the air. These aerial rivers, let us not pollute their currents. What meadows do they course through? How many fine mails there are which **traverse** their routes! He is privileged who gets his letter **franked** by them.

I believe these things.
Henry. D. Thoreau

像是诸神手中的工具。心里装着这样宽宏的信任，有什么难关是过不去的呢？然而我们所面临的最大的危害就是没有信仰。没有一根羽毛，或者一根稻草，是被托付了这种信任的；那个包裹是空的。只有我们才被上帝托以这种信任，事实上，我们是所有事物的代理人。

我久久不能忘怀的就是这样的善意，无须言语表达。话还没从对方口中说出来，我就已经明白了，不用多说。对此，上帝不可能会错意，人也无法用言语来解释。我们的交流就像地下的狐狸洞穴，不见天日，寂静无声。只有信念和爱才能发现我们。自然中，被认为是空空如也的地方，比起堆满了土石的地方，要丰富得多！——是因为流动不息的大自然的影响。除了这样，我们难道还有别的交流方式吗？我们的心灵比大自然更厌恶真空。一股股潮流刺穿空气的毛孔，在空气中流动穿行。我们不要污染它们了吧。它们流经的是什么样的草地呢？它们又传送着人们多少美妙的信啊！要是谁的信件能以这种方式免费寄送出去，那他真是幸运至极。

这就是我所相信的。

亨利·大卫·梭罗
1843年2月12日

单词解析 *Word Analysis*

tarry ['tæri] *vi.* 逗留；耽搁

例 I saw no reason to tarry in that country.
我看不出要滞留在那国家的理由。

trivial ['trɪviəl] *adj.* 琐碎的，无价值的

例 My mind attempted to calm itself by fastening on this trivial detail.
我尝试将注意力集中在这个小细节上以让自己平静下来。

dynamically [daɪ'næmɪklɪ] *adj.* 精力充沛的，有干劲的

例 Germany has a dynamically growing market at home.
德国国内市场持续增长。

transpire [træn'spaɪə(r)] *v.* 发生

例 Nothing is known as yet about what transpired at the meeting.
会上到底发生了什么现在还没人知道。

confide [kən'faɪd] *v.* 吐露（或倾诉）秘密

例 I knew she had some fundamental problems in her marriage because she had confided in me a year earlier.
我知道她的婚姻存在一些根本性的问题，早在一年前她就向我倾诉过。

reciprocal [rɪ'sɪprəkl] *adj.* 互相的；相应的；互惠的

例 Both sides had reciprocally observed restraints.
双方都遵守了限制性规定。

strait [streɪt] *n.* （常用复数）困境，境况窘迫

例 She found herself in desperate financial straits.
她发觉自己经济状况极为窘迫。

intrust [ɪn'trʌst] *vt.* 信托，交托

例 There are few people in the company intrusted by him, except Tom.
除了汤姆，他在公司没有什么信赖的人。

burrow ['bʌrəʊ] *n.* 地洞

例 As soon as the two chicks hatch, they leave the nest burrow.

Henry David Thoreau to Ralph Waldo Emerson
亨利·大卫·梭罗致拉尔夫·瓦尔多·爱默生

两只小鸟一出壳就离开了巢穴。

traverse [trəˈvɜːs] *vt.* 横穿；横越；穿过
- 例 I traversed the narrow pedestrian bridge.
  我走过狭窄的人行天桥。

frank [fræŋk] *vt.* 免费寄（邮件）
- 例 The letter was franked in London on August 6.
  这封信 8 月 6 日在伦敦盖过免费邮戳。

语法知识点 Grammar Points

① **As the packet still tarries, I will send you some thoughts, which I have lately relearned, as the latest public and private news.**

这个句子中第一个"as"引导原因状语从句，第二个"as"是介词，表示"作为……"。
- 例 He was awarded a medal as his prize of winning the game.
  他赢了比赛，被授予一个奖牌作为奖励。

② **Perhaps it is only essential to friendship that some vital trust should have been reposed by the one in the other.**

这个句子中"it"为形式主语，真正的主语为"that"引导的从句，也就是主语从句。在这个句子中，因为"that"引导的从句太长，所以放在句子后面，避免句子头重脚轻。
- 例 It is dangerous that Daniel plays computer games all day and night.
  丹尼尔没日没夜地玩电脑游戏是危险的。

③ **Nothing sensible passes between.**

这个句子中"nothing"为不定代词，形容词"sensible"放在其后，是因为形容词修饰不定代词时均须放在其后。
- 例 There is nothing special about his painting, just imitation of Da Vinci.
  他的画没什么特别的，就是模仿达·芬奇而已。

经典名句 *Famous Classics*

1. Rather than love, than money, than fame, give me truth. — *Walden*
   不必给我爱，不必给我钱，不必给我名誉，给我真理吧。——《瓦尔登湖》

2. Life comes with a certain talent. — Ralph Waldo Emerson
   人生来就具有一定的天赋。——爱默生

3. A man is rich in proportion to the number of things which he can afford to let alone. — *Walden*
   一个人越是有许多事情能够放得下，他越是富有。——《瓦尔登湖》

4. Ignorant is not free, because his opposition is a strange world. — Schopenhauer
   无知者是不自由的，正因和他对立的是一个陌生的世界。——叔本华

5. Only those who never look up at the stars, will not fall into the pit. — Thales
   只有那些从不仰望星空的人，才不会跌入坑中。——古希腊思想家泰勒斯

6. The Transformers teaches us that things are not always what they appear to be. — *The Big Bang Theory*
   变形金刚的故事告诉我们，事情的真相往往与其外在表现不同。——《生活大爆炸》

7. Sometimes one pays most for the things one gets for nothing. — Albert Einstein
   有时候一个人为不花钱得到的东西付出的代价最高。——爱因斯坦

8. All nature is but art, unknown to thee, — Pope
   整个自然都是艺术，这是你所不知的。——蒲柏

15 Theodore Roosevelt to Theodore Roosevelt Jr.
西奥多·罗斯福致小西奥多·罗斯福

White House, October 2, 1905

Blessed Old Ted,

The thing to do is to go on just as what you have evidently been doing, attract as little attention as possible, and do not make a **fuss** about the newspaper men, camera creatures, and idiots generally, letting it be seen that you do not like them and avoid them, but not letting them betray you into any excessive irritation. I believe they will soon drop you, and it is just an unpleasant thing that you will have to **live down**. Ted, I have had an enormous number of unpleasant things that I have had to live down in my life at different times and you have begun to have them now. I saw that you were not out on the football field on Saturday and was rather glad of it, as evidently those **infernal** idiots were eagerly waiting for you, but whenever you do go you will have to make up your mind that they will make it exceedingly unpleasant for you for once or twice, and you will just have to bear it, for you can never in the world afford to

福儿泰德：

你现在应该做的就是和以前一样，吸引尽可能少的注意力，不要对记者和照相的人大惊小怪，他们通常都是一群傻瓜，你要表现出对他们的厌恶并躲避他们，但不要对他们恼羞成怒、大发雷霆。我相信他们很快就会对你失去兴趣，这只是你要努力忘掉的不愉快的事情之一。泰德，在我的生命中的各个阶段，都有很多我要设法忘记的不愉快的事情。现在，你也开始遇到这些事情了。周六，我在橄榄球场没有见到你的身影，对此，我感到非常高兴。因为那些从地狱来的傻瓜笨蛋们蹲守在那儿，就等着你出现呢。但是，无论你什么时候去，你都要明白：他们一次或者两次会让你感到极其的不愉快，这是你必须要忍耐的。因为你绝不能因为厌恶记者的追踪就放弃想要做的事情，无论是橄榄球还是其他。

let them drive you away from anything you intend to do, whether it is football or anything else, and by going about your own business quietly and pleasantly, doing just what you would do as if they were not there, generally they will get tired of it, and the boys themselves will see that it is not your fault, and feel, if anything, rather a sympathy for you. Meanwhile I want you to know that we are all thinking of you and sympathizing with you the whole time; and it is a great comfort to me to have such confidence in you and to know that though these creatures can cause you a little trouble and make you feel a little **downcast**, they cannot drive you one way or the other, or make you alter the course you have set out for yourself.

We were all of us, I am almost ashamed to say, rather blue at getting back in the White House, simply because we missed Sagamore Hill so much. But it is very beautiful and we feel very ungrateful at having even a passing fit of blueness, and we are enjoying it to the full now. I have just seen Archie dragging some fifty foot of hose pipe across the tennis court to play in the **sand-box**. I have been playing tennis with Mr. Pinchot, who beat me three sets to one, the only deuce-set being the one I won.

只要你默默地享受着要做的事，和平常一样，就好像记者不在旁边似的，通常记者们会变得厌烦，球员们也会明白这不是你的过错，如果有任何感想的话，只会对你表示同情。与此同时我要告诉你的是我们都在想着你，都很同情你。我对你有信心，知道虽然记者和拍照者们会给你带来一些麻烦，让你精神低迷，但你不会被他们牵着走，不会改变自己的人生轨迹，这让我很宽慰。

难以启齿的是，我们大家回到白宫后都很失落，因为太过想念酋长山。但是白宫很漂亮，只要有忧郁的念头闪过，我们就会感到自己不懂得感恩，所以现在我们完全适应了白宫的生活。刚刚我看见阿奇拖着个50英尺长的水管穿过网球场，去玩沙箱了。我和平肖先生刚才一直在打网球，他3:1胜了我，唯一有盘末平分的就是我胜的那一盘。

这正是一个展现你的素质的机会。不要受新闻业人员的影响，不要偏离你在橄榄球场或其他方面的既定路线，一丝一毫也不行。尽可能不要小题大做，以免陷入混乱。

1905年10月2日于白宫

Theodore Roosevelt to Theodore Roosevelt Jr.
西奥多·罗斯福致小西奥多·罗斯福

This is just an occasion to show the stuff what there is in you. Do not let these newspaper creatures and **kindred** idiots drive you on hair's breadth from the line you had marked out in football or anything else. Avoid any fuss, if possible.

单词解析 Word Analysis

fuss [fʌs] *n.* 无谓的激动（或忧虑、活动）；大惊小怪

例 I don't know why everybody makes such a fuss about a few mosquitoes.
我不知道为什么大家对几只蚊子大惊小怪的。

live down 改正行为而使……被人遗忘

例 James is still trying to live down the excitement he caused when he broke the window.
詹姆斯还在努力使人忘记他打碎了窗子时所造成的骚动。

infernal [ɪnˈfɜːnl] *adj.* 地狱的；阴间的；可恶的

例 They can't work in these infernal conditions.
他们不能在这样糟糕透顶的条件下工作。

downcast [ˈdaʊnkɑːst] *adj.* 悲哀的；沮丧的

例 Since their defeat last time, the enemy have become really downcast.
自从上次遭到挫败，敌军变得很颓靡。

sand-box 沙箱；沙盒

例 Tom went to the beach but couldn't find his sand-box anymore.
汤姆去了沙滩，但是找不到他的沙盒了。

kindred [ˈkɪndrəd] *adj.* 类似的；相似的

例 I recall many discussions with her on these and kindred topics.
我回想起多次同她就这些问题及类似话题进行的讨论。

语法知识点 Grammar Points

① **The thing to do is to go on just as you have evidently been doing, attract as little attention as possible, do not make a fuss about the newspaper men, camera creatures, and idiots generally, letting it be seen that you do not like them and avoid them, but not letting them betray you into any excessive irritation.**

这个句子中"letting"是"let"的现在分词，在这里做状语表目的。

例 They went to the church, praying for people who died in the war.
他们去教堂为在战争中死去的人祈祷。

② **But whenever you do go you will have to make up your mind that they will make it exceedingly unpleasant for you for once or twice, and you will just have to bear it.**

这个句子中"whenever you do go"是"无论什么时候你真的去（橄榄球场）"的意思，其中"do"后可以跟动词原形，表示强调，意为"一定、确实"。

例 I do apologize for what my son has done to you.
我真的要为我儿子对你所做的事情道歉。

③ **I have been playing tennis with Mr. Pinchot, who beat me three sets to one, the only deuce-set being the one I won.**

这个句子中"the only deuce-set being the one I won"是一个独立主格，表示对主句发生的事情进行补充说明。

例 A bird standing on his shoulder, the merchant walked into the bar.
这个商人走进了酒吧，肩膀上还站着一只小鸟。

经典名句 Famous Classics

1. Believe you can and you're halfway there. — Theodore Roosevelt
   相信自己能做到，你就已经成功了一半。——西奥多·罗斯福（美国总统）

2. Endurance and persist; this pain will turn to your good by and by.
   — Ovid

忍受和坚持，这种痛苦将逐渐变得对你有利。——奥维德

3. Character is what you are in the dark. — D. L Moody
   暗处最能反映一个人真正品格。——美国教士 穆迪.D.L

4. Life is just a series of trying to make up your mind. — T. Fuller
   生活只是由一系列下决心的努力所构成的。——富勒

5. Man is the artificer of his own happiness. — Proverb
   人之幸福，自己创造。——英国谚语

6. Rudeness is merely an expression of fear. — *The Grand Budapest Hotel*
   无礼只是恐惧的一种表露。——《布达佩斯大饭店》

7. I fear the worst too, because fearing the best is a complete waste of time. — *Happy Feet*
   我也害怕最糟的情况可能会发生，因为害怕最好的会发生完全是在浪费时间。——《快乐的大脚》

8. What is an ocean but a multitude of drops? — *Cloud Atlas*
   没有无数的水滴，又怎么汇聚成汪洋江海？——《云图》

读书笔记

16 David Hume to Adam Smith
大卫·休谟致亚当·斯密

Edinburgh, Jack's Land, 26 May 1753

My Dear Sir,

I was very sorry to hear by Mr. Leechman that you had been ill **of late**. I am afraid the **fatigues** of your class have exhausted you too much, and that you require more leisure and rest than you allow yourself. However, the good season and the vacation now approaches; and I hope you intend, both for exercise and relaxation, to take a **jaunt** to this place. I have many things to communicate to you. Were you not my friend, you would envy my **robust constitution**. My **application** has been and is continual; and yet I preserve entire health. I am now beginning the Long Parliament; which, considering the great number of volumes I **peruse**, and my **scrupulous** method of composing, I regard as a very great advance I think you should settle in this town during the vacation; where there is always some good **company**; and you know, that I can supply you with books, as many as you want please.

亲爱的先生：

我从里奇曼先生那里听到了您最近身体不太好的消息，对此我非常难过。我担心，是您的教学工作太累人，因此您需要的放松和休息恐怕比你允许的要多得多。不过，美好的季节和假期已经临近，我希望您不管是出于锻炼还是放松的目的，来我这里做一次短途旅行吧。我有很多话要跟您说。如果不是我的朋友的话，我强健的体格会让您感到嫉妒的。我还是在一如既往地勤奋工作，而且身体也没有出什么毛病。我现在开始写"长期议会"时期的历史了，考虑到我有那么多的文献要读，我的编写方法又那么严谨，我认为您来这里度假对我会有很大的好处。这里不缺少能和您聊得来的同伴，还有，您知道的，我能给您提供很多书，您可以随意翻阅。

请求您在有空的时候务必

I beg to hear from you at your Leisure; and I am

   Your affectionate friend and humble
           Servant
           David Hume

给我回信。

您亲爱的朋友和谦逊的仆人
大卫·休谟
1753年5月26日于爱丁堡杰克兰

单词解析 Word Analysis

of late 近来，最近

例 As you'll have read in our news pages, all has not been well of late.
正如你会从我们的新闻版面中看到的一样，最近一切都不太顺利。

fatigue [fəˈtiːg] *n.* 疲劳，疲乏

例 Fatigue and stress quickly result in a dull complexion and a furrowed brow.
疲劳和压力会很快导致肤色暗淡无光、额头出现皱纹。

jaunt [dʒɔːnt] *n.* （短途）游览

例 Shopping online is more of a necessity than convenience, though a two-hour jaunt to Memphis is common.
网上购物并不是为了方便，而是着实有必要，尽管花费两个小时去孟菲斯的短程购物之旅也是很普遍的选择。

robust [rəʊˈbʌst] *adj.* 强健的；强壮的

例 To judge from his productivity, Mozart clearly enjoyed robust good health throughout his twenties.
从创作能力来看，莫扎特20~30岁时显然精力充沛，身体健康。

constitution [ˌkɒnstɪˈtjuːʃn] *n.* 身体素质；体质；体格

例 He must have an extremely strong constitution.
他的体格必定极其强壮。

application [ˌæplɪˈkeɪʃn] *n.* 勤奋；努力

例 Success as a writer demands great application.
作家要成功就得悉力以赴。

peruse [pəˈruːz] *vt.* 研读；细读

例 She found the information while she was perusing a copy of *Life* magazine.
她在读《生活》杂志的时候看到了这个消息。

scrupulous [ˈskruːpjələs] *adj.* 仔细的；细致的；一丝不苟的

例 The Board is scrupulous in its consideration of all applications for licenses.
委员会对所有申请许可证的人予以审慎考虑。

company [ˈkʌmpəni] *n.* 同伴，朋友

例 My cat Gustaf was the only thing I had — the only company.
我的猫古斯塔夫是我所有的一切——我唯一的伴侣。

语法知识点 *Grammar Points*

① Were you not my friend, you would envy my robust Constitution.

这个句子用到了虚拟语气，主句为"you would..."，从句是一个省略了"if"的条件状语从句"were you..."。虚拟语气中，"if"引导的条件状语从句中出现"were、had、should"时，这三个词可提前至句首，同时"if"也可省略。

例 Should it not snow tomorrow, we couldn't make a snowman.
明天要是不下雪，我们就不能堆雪人了。

② I am now beginning the Long Parliament; which, considering the great number of volumes I peruse, and my scrupulous method of composing, I regard as a very great advance I think you should settle in this town during the vacation.

这个句子中"considering"是动词的现在分词做介词的用法，意为"考虑到"。同样用法的还有"regarding（关于）""concerning（关于）""saving（除……之外）"等。

例 Saving a few slices of ham, we had eaten nothing all day.
除了几片火腿，我们一整天都没吃东西。

经典名句 Famous Classics

1. The world is a book, but people who do not travel read only one page. — Augustinus
   世界是一本书，而不旅行的人们只读了其中的一页。——奥古斯狄尼斯

2. Reading is the stillness of the tourism. Tourism is the mobile reading. — Proverb
   读书是静止的旅游，旅游是移动的阅读。——谚语

3. To travel hopefully is a better thing than to arrive, and the true success is to labor. — Robert Louis Stevenson
   怀着希望去旅行比抵达目的地更愉快；而真正的成功在于工作。——史蒂文森

4. The road to a friend's house is never long. — Danish proverb
   去朋友家的路总不嫌长。——丹麦谚语

5. All work and no play makes Jack a dull boy. — Proverb
   只学习，不玩耍，聪明的孩子也变傻。——谚语

6. People who cannot find time for recreation are obliged sooner or later to find time for illness.
   没有时间娱乐的人,迟早得有时间生病。

7. If you don't walk out, you will think that this is the whole world. — *Nuovo Cinema Paradiso*
   如果你不出去走走，你就会以为这就是全世界。——《天堂电影院》

8. I love waking up in the morning and not knowing what's going to happen, or who I'm going to meet, where I am going to wind up. — *Titanic*
   我喜欢早上一起来时一切都是未知的，不知会遇见什么人，会有什么样的结局。——《泰坦尼克号》

17 Adam Smith to William Strahan
亚当·斯密致威廉·斯特拉恩

Kirkaldy, Fifeshire, 9 November 1776

...Thus died our most excellent, and never to be forgotten friend; concerning whose philosophical opinions men will, no doubt, judge variously, every one approving or **condemning** them, **according as** they happen to coincide or disagree with his own; but concerning whose character and conduct there can scarce be a difference of opinion. His temper, indeed, seemed to be more happily balanced, if I may be allowed such an expression, than that perhaps of any other man I have ever known. Even in the lowest state of his fortune, his great and necessary frugality never hindered him from exercising, upon proper occasions, acts both of charity and generosity. It was a **frugality** founded, not upon **avarice**, but upon the love of independency. The extreme gentleness of his nature never weakened either the firmness of his mind, or the steadiness of his resolutions. His constant pleasantry was the genuine **effusion** of good-nature and good-

……就这样，我们最杰出的、铭记在心的朋友去世了。毫无疑问，对他的哲学思想的评价是不一而足的，人们赞同与自己思想相符的、贬低与自己思想不符的。但是，对他的品行却很难有不同的看法。说真的，他的性情是我见过的人里面——如果我能这么描述的话——最刚柔并济的。即使最窘迫的时候，尽管自己省吃俭用，但在适当的场合下还是对别人十分慷慨仁慈。他的节俭不是因为贪财，而是对独立的热爱。他温和的性格从没有让他的头脑失去定力，也不会使他的决心动摇。他的妙语连珠是好性情和幽默感的自然表达，与他温恭谦逊的态度也密不可分，并且不带丝毫恶意。有的人所谓的机智正来源于这令人不快的恶意。他的打趣从来不是想要羞辱别人，因此，他从不会冒犯别人，反而总是让听的人感到愉快和

humor, **tempered** with delicacy and modesty, and without even the slightest **tincture** of **malignity**, so frequently the disagreeable source of what is called wit in other men. It never was the meaning of his **raillery** to mortify; and therefore, far from offending, it seldom failed to please and delight even those who were the objects of it. To his friends, who were frequently the objects of it, there was not perhaps any one of all his great and amiable qualities, which contributed more to endear his conversation. And that **gaiety** of temper, so agreeable in society, but which is so often accompanied with **frivolous** and superficial qualities, was in him certainly attended with the most severe application, the most extensive learning, the greatest depth of thought, and a capacity in every respect the most comprehensive. Upon the whole, I have always considered him, both in his lifetime and since his death, as approaching as nearly to the idea of a perfectly wise and virtuous man, as perhaps the nature of frailty will permit.

I ever am, dear sir,
Most affectionately yours,
Adam Smith

好笑，就算是被打趣了的对象也是如此。对他经常打趣的朋友而言，他所有亲切和蔼的品质都比不上这一点能让他的谈话更有魅力。像他这样欢快的性格，在社会交往中十分受欢迎，往往又带着些轻浮、浅薄。但是在他身上，却与专注的工作态度、渊博的学识、深邃的思想以及不断学习接受各种学问的能力融为一体。总体上，不论在他生前还是死后，我都一直把他当作人类脆弱的天性所能达到的范围内德才兼备的、最接近完美的人。

亲爱的先生，
永远是您最亲爱的
亚当·斯密
1776年11月9日
于法夫郡柯尔卡迪

单词解析 Word Analysis

condemn [kən'dem] v. 谴责；指责

例 Graham was right to condemn his players for lack of ability, attitude and application.
格雷厄姆指责队员们技艺不佳、态度不端正而且不够努力，他说得没错。

according as 依据，按照

例 According as my teacher said, Mary had passed the test.
据我的老师说，玛丽已经通过了考试。

frugality [frʊ'gæləti] n. 节约，朴素，节俭

例 Industry and frugality are the inherent qualities of the Chinese nation.
勤劳俭朴是中华民族的本色。

avarice ['ævərɪs] n. 贪婪

例 Avarice is the bane to happiness.
贪婪是损毁幸福的祸根。

effusion [ɪ'fjuːʒn] n. （感情）过分流露，迸发

例 His employer greeted him with an effusion of relief.
他的雇主看到他大松一口气。

temper ['tempə(r)] v. 调剂，调和

例 She asked the court to temper justice with mercy.
她请求法庭法外开恩。

tincture ['tɪŋktʃə(r)] n. 色泽，气息

例 I'd say he is a man who has the least tincture of learning.
我认为他是一个最没有学术气味的人。

malignity [mə'lɪgnɪti] n. 极度的恶意，恶毒

例 This has, in a great degree, been produced by the violence and malignity of party spirit.
这一切，很大程度上是暴力和恶毒党争的结果。

raillery ['reɪləri] *n.* 善意的嘲笑；逗趣

例 There was a certain amount of raillery at Joe's expense.
有些笑话是在拿乔寻开心。

endear [ɪn'dɪə(r)] *vt.* 使受喜爱

例 He has endeared himself to the American public.
他已经赢得了美国民众的好感。

gaiety ['geɪəti] *n.* 快乐；愉快；高兴

例 The colourful flags added to the gaiety of the occasion.
彩旗增添了盛会的欢乐气氛。

frivolous ['frɪvələs] *adj.* 轻浮的；轻佻的

例 Inclination in that direction has long been considered frivolous and unmanly.
这方面的爱好长期被认为是轻薄和非男子气的。

语法知识点 *Grammar Points*

Concerning whose philosophical opinions men will, no doubt, judge variously, every one approving or condemning them, according as they happen to coincide or disagree with his own.

这个句子中"every one approving or condemning..."是一个独立主格结构，因为"every one"是动作发出者，所以"approve"和"condemn"均用现在分词形式。

例 Tom's sister was painting, he washing the brushes for her.
汤姆的妹妹在画油画，汤姆就为她洗刷子。

经典名句 *Famous Classics*

1. Adventure is a state of mind – and spirit. It comes with faith, for with complete faith, there is no fear of what faces you in life or death. — Jacqueline Cochran
冒险是一种心态，一种精神。它来自信念，因为有了绝对的信念，你

将不再有恐惧，无论生或死。——贾桂琳·科克伦（飞行员）

2. I never consider a difference of opinion in politics, in religion, in philosophy, as cause for withdrawing from a friend. — Thomas Jefferson
我从不认为政治、宗教及哲理上的意见分歧，能够成为离开朋友的理由。——托马斯·杰斐逊（美国第三任总统）

3. In religion and politics, people's beliefs and convictions are in almost every case gotten at second hand, and without examination. — Mark Twain
在宗教及政治，人们的信仰及信念几乎在所有场合里都是二手取来的，没有经过自己仔细的检视。——马克·吐温

4. With every deed you are sowing a seed, though the harvest you may not see. — Ella Wheeler Wilcox, Poet
你的每一个行为都是在播种，即使你还没见到收成。——艾拉·惠勒·威尔克斯（诗人）

5. Good management consists in showing average people how to do the work of superior people. — John D. Rockefeller
好的管理主要在于展现一般人如何做杰出人所做的事。——约翰·洛克菲勒（工业家）

6. Meet success like a gentleman and disaster like a man. — Winston Churchill
像绅士般面对成功，像男人般面对灾祸。——温斯顿·丘吉尔（英国首相）

7. I do not think there is any thrill that can go through the human heart like that felt by the inventor as he sees some creation of the brain unfolding to success. — Nikola Tesla, Inventor
比起发明者看到脑里的想象逐渐实现并取得成功，我觉得没有什么可以让人心如此兴奋。——尼古拉·特斯拉（发明家）

8. For success, attitude is equally as important as ability. — Walter Scott, Novelist
为取得成功，态度与能力一样重要。——华特·司各特（小说家）

18 Francis Scott Fitzgerald to Ernest Hemingway
弗朗西斯·斯科特·菲茨杰拉德致欧内斯特·海明威

December 23, 1926

Dear Ernest,

Your letter **depressed** me—illogically because I knew **more or less** what was coming. I wish I could have seen you and heard you, if you wished, give some sort of version of what happened to you. Anyhow I'm sorry for you and for Hadley and for Bumby and I hope someway you'll all be **content** and things will not seem so hard and bad.

I can't tell you how much your friendship has meant to me during this year and a half—It is the brightest thing in our trip to Europe for me. I will try to look out for your interests with Scribner's in America, but I **gather** that the need of that is past now and that soon you'll be **financially** more than on your feet.

I'm sorry you didn't come to Marseille. I go back with my novel still unfinished and with less health and not much more money than when I came, but somehow content, for the moment,

亲爱的欧内斯特：

收到你的信让我没有来由地十分沮丧，因为我或多或少知道一些将要发生的事情。我多希望能见到你并且听你讲讲发生的事情啊，如果你愿意的话。不管怎样，我为你、哈德利（海明威第一任妻子，译注）和邦比（海明威长子，译注）感到遗憾，希望你们能有满意的结果，情况不再这么困难和糟糕。

我无法告诉你在这一年半的时间里我们的友情对我有多么重要——对我而言，它是我们的欧洲之旅中最美好的事物。我会尽力照看好你在美国思科伯里纳公司的利益，但是我想这很快就不需要了，因为不久你在经济上会更加独立。

我很遗憾你没来马赛。此次回美国，我的小说还没写完，身体也变差了，身上的钱也不比来时多，但是眼下不

with motion and New York ahead and Zelda's entire recovery—and happy about the amount of my book that I've already written.

I'm delighted with what press I've already seen of *The Sun Also Rises*, etc. Did not realize that you had stolen it all from me but am prepared to believe that it's true and shall tell everyone. By the way I liked it in print even better than in **manuscript**.

1st printing was probably 5,000. 2nd printing may mean that they've sold 4,500 so have ordered up 3,000 more. It may mean any sale from 2,500 to 5,000, though.

College Humor pays fine. No movie in *The Sun Also Rises* unless book is big success of **scandal**. That's just a guess.

We all enjoyed La vie est beau avec Papa. We agree with Bumby.

Always yours affectionately,
Scott

知怎么的，回国的旅途、就在前方的纽约和完全恢复了的泽尔达（菲茨杰拉德的妻子，译注）让我觉得很满足——还有对已写完的书也很满意。

看过了《太阳照常升起》等书的校样后，我感到很高兴。之前没有意识到你都是从我这里偷去的，现在我十分愿意相信这是真的，还要告诉每一个人。还有，比起手稿，我更喜欢它的印刷本。

第一次印刷可能是5000册，第二次印刷可能意味着已经卖出去了4500本，所以要加印3000本。不过，这可能意味着卖出去的数量在2500到5000之间。

《学院幽默》稿酬不错。除非《太阳照常升起》成功揭露各种各样的丑闻，否则它不会被改编成电影。我只是这么猜测而已。

我们都很喜欢《和爸爸在一起的生活真美好》（可能是海明威之子邦比的一篇作文，译注），我们都很同意邦比的观点。

永远是你亲爱的，
斯科特
1926年12月23日

Francis Scott Fitzgerald to Ernest Hemingway
弗朗西斯·斯科特·菲茨杰拉德致欧内斯特·海明威

单词解析 Word Analysis

depress [dɪ'pres] *vt.* 使抑郁；使沮丧

例 Mary's passing away depressed him for a long time.
他为玛丽的去世难过了很久。

more or less 或多或少地

例 His success has more or less to do with his wife's support.
他的成功多多少少离不开他妻子的支持。

content ['kɒntent] *adj.* 满足的，满意的

例 Not content with rescuing one theatre, Sally Green has taken on another.
萨莉·格林不满足于挽救一家剧院，她又接手了另外一家。

gather ['gæðə(r)] *vt.* 认为；猜想

例 I gather from your E-mail that you're not enjoying your job.
我从邮件中了解到你并不喜欢你的工作。

financially [fə'nænʃəlɪ] *adv.* 财政上，金融上，经济上

例 Jennifer believes she will move out on her own when she is financially able to support herself
珍妮弗相信，当自己有钱养活自己时，就会搬出去单住。

manuscript ['mænjuskrɪpt] *n.* 手稿；原稿

例 The manuscript had already been sent off to the printers.
原稿已经寄给印刷厂了。

scandal ['skændl] *n.* 丑闻；流言蜚语

例 After the scandal was exposed, Dr Bailey committed suicide.
丑闻曝光后，贝利博士自杀了。

语法知识点 Grammar Points

① I will try to look out for your interests with Scribner's in America, but I gather that the need of that is past now and that soon you'll be financially more than on your feet.

这个句子是一个由"but"连接的并列句，第二个分句中有两个由"that"引导的宾语从句，第一个从句的引导词"that"可省略，第二个"that"不可省略。

例 My teacher always told us we should study hard and that we must not copy others' work.
我的老师总是告诉我们要好好学习，而且不能抄袭别人的作品。

② **I go back with my novel still unfinished and with less health and not much more money than when I came.**

这个句子中"with my novel unfinished"是"with + n. + adj./ adv./ prep./ 动词现在分词/动词过去分词"的用法，在这里做伴随状语。

例 She came to my house with a book written by her.
她带着她写的一本书来我家。

经典名句 *Famous Classics*

1. Good friends and advice can foster virtues. — Francois Rabelais
   益友和良言能培养人的美德。——拉伯雷（作家）

2. Friendship is based on comrade, consolidate on sincere, development in criticism, terminate in flattery.
   友谊建立在同志中，巩固在真挚上，发展在批评里，断送在奉承中。

3. True friendship is sincere and bold.
   真正的友谊是诚挚的和大胆的。

4. A friend is one who knows us, but loves us anyway. — Fr. Jerome Cummings.
   朋友就是那些了解我们，但依然爱我们的人。——Fr·杰罗姆·卡敏斯

5. True friend is one who overlooks your failures and tolerates your successes. — English proverb
   真正的朋友从不追究你的过错，也从不妒忌你的成功。——英文谚语

6. A friend to everybody is a friend to nobody.
   广交友，无深交。

7. He that lies down with dogs must rise up with fleas.

近朱者赤，近墨者黑。

8. No man is the whole of himself; his friends are the rest of him. — H. E. Fosdick
   没有人是十全十美的，朋友补充了他的不足。——福斯迪克（美国牧师）

读书笔记

19 Adam Smith to David Hume
亚当·斯密致大卫·休谟

September 1765

My Dear Friend,

It gives me the greatest pleasure to find that you are so well contented with your present situation. I think however you are wrong in thinking of settling at Paris. A man is always **displaced** in a foreign country, and notwithstanding the boasted humanity and politeness of this nation, they appear to me to be, in general, more meanly interested, and that the **cordiality** of their friendship is much less to be depended on than that of our own countrymen. They live in such large **societies** and their affections are **dissipated** among so great a variety of objects, that they can bestow but a very small share of them upon any individual. Do not imagine that the great Princes and Ladies who want you to live with them make this proposal from real and sincere affection to you. They mean nothing but to gratify their own vanity by having an **illustrious** man in their house, and you would soon feel the want of that cordial and trusty affection

我亲爱的朋友：

你对自己的现状感到满意，对我来说是极大的快乐。但是我不赞同你想在巴黎定居的打算。身处异国不免有背井离乡之感；而且尽管法国以人道和礼貌著称，但在我眼里，这些礼貌和人道大体上更是一种低级趣味；法国人对朋友的热忱比起我们的国人来说更不可靠。他们的社交圈子太大了，他们对朋友的关爱被分散到了各式各样的人身上，导致他们只能把很少的关爱分给任何一个单独的人。不要以为邀请你同住的王公和贵妇们是出于对你真心实意的喜爱。他们想要的不过是让自己的家里住着一位有名望的人，以此满足他们的虚荣心。你很快就会怀念曾在赫特福德勋爵和夫人家里受到的真诚又可靠的关爱了。请代我向勋爵和夫人致以郑重和充满敬意的问候。

在我看来，你对伦敦的

which you enjoyed in the family of Lord and Lady Hertford, to whom I must beg to be remembered in the most **dutiful** and respectful manner.

Your objections to London appear to me to be without foundation. The hatred of Scothmen can **subsist**, even at present, among nobody but the stupidest of the People, and is such a piece of **nonsense** that it must fall even among them in a twelvemonth. The **clamour** against you on account of **deism** is stronger, no doubt, at London where you are a native and consequently may be a candidate for everything, than at Paris where as a foreigner, you possibly can be a candidate for nothing. Your presence dissipated in six months time much stronger prejudices in Edinburgh, and when you appear at Court, in open day light, as you must do upon your return, and not live **obscurely** at Miss Elliot's with six or seven Scotchmen as before, the same irresistible good temper will in a very few weeks dissipate much weaker prejudices at London and **hold their tongues**.

In short I have a very great interest in your settling at London, where, after many firm resolutions to return to Scotland, I think it is most likely I shall settle myself. Let us make short excursions together sometimes to see our

不满是没有根据的。对苏格兰人的仇视，即使是现在，也只存在于最愚蠢的人中间；这种仇视又是如此的没有道理以至于愚蠢的人在一年之内也会改观。毫无疑问，由于自然神论而反对你的吵嚷声在伦敦比在巴黎要大得多，因为在伦敦你是本地人，有权利参与各项事务，但在巴黎你是外来者，几乎什么事情都无权参与。在爱丁堡，你在六个月内就驱散了人们对你的强烈偏见。如果你光明正大地出席法庭，正如你回来后必须立即做的那样，而不是像以前一样和六七个苏格兰人隐居在埃利奥特小姐的公寓里，你那无往而不胜的好性情会在几周内就驱散伦敦的居民对你的微弱偏见，将闲言碎语平息下来的。

简言之，我非常希望你能定居在伦敦，这里是我尽管在多次下定决心回苏格兰之后，非常可能定居的地方。我们可以一起偶尔做个短途旅行去看望我们在法国和苏格兰的朋友，但是让伦敦成为我们日常的住地吧……

1765年9月

friends in France and sometimes to see our friends in Scotland, but let London be the place of our ordinary residence...

单词解析 *Word Analysis*

displace [dɪsˈpleɪs] *vt.* 迫使……迁徙；迫使……背井离乡

- Most of the civilians displaced by the war will be unable to return to their homes.
  许多因战乱而流离失所的百姓将无法重返家园。

cordiality [ˌkɔːdɪˈælətɪ] *n.* 热诚，诚挚

- My father greeted me with unexpected cordiality.
  我的父亲以出乎意外的热诚迎接我。

society [səˈsaɪətɪ] *n.* 社交界，社交

- The event has astonished London society.
  这一事件震惊了伦敦的社交界。

dissipate [ˈdɪsɪpeɪt] *vt.* 驱散；消散

- He wound down the windows to dissipate the heat.
  他摇下窗子来散热。

illustrious [ɪˈlʌstrɪəs] *adj.* 著名的；杰出的；卓越的

- Premier Zhou's illustrious deeds are an everlasting monument in the hearts of the Chinese people.
  周总理的光辉业绩在中国人民心中立下了不朽的丰碑。

dutiful [ˈdjuːtɪfl] *adj.* 尽职的；恭敬顺从的

- The days of the dutiful wife, who sacrifices her career for her husband, are over.
  贤妻为了丈夫而牺牲自己事业的时代已经结束了。

subsist [səbˈsɪst] *vi.* 存在；有效

- The living things on the earth could not subsist on Mars.
  地球上的生物不可能在火星上生存。

nonsense ['nɒnsns] *n.* 胡闹；胡说

例 Surely it is an economic nonsense to deplete the world of natural resources.
耗尽世界的自然资源毋庸置疑是愚蠢的经济行为。

clamour ['klæmə(r)] *n.* 喧哗声，喧闹

例 A great clamour has arisen around the question of peace or war.
是和是战，闹得甚嚣尘上。

deism ['deɪɪzəm] *n.* 自然神论

例 Voltaire's religion thoughts were a trinity of anti-church, deism and tolerant of religious.
伏尔泰的宗教思想是反教会、自然神论、宗教宽容三位一体。

obscurely [əb'skjʊəlɪ] *adv.* 不引人注意地，隐匿地

例 He does not satisfy himself with writing stories obscurely any longer.
他不再满足于隐姓埋名地写故事了。

hold one's tongue 保持沉默；绝口不谈

例 He pointed out many problems in our plan, but when it came to solutions, he held his tongue.
他指出了我们计划中的很多问题，但谈到解决办法时，他就不作声了。

语法知识点 *Grammar Points*

① **A man is always displaced in a foreign Country, and notwithstanding the boasted humanity and politeness of this Nation, they appear to me to be, in general, more meanly interested, and that the cordiality of their friendship is much less to be depended on than that of our own countrymen.**

这个句子是一个并列句，由第一个"and"分隔开来。在后一个并列分句中用到了比较级，比较的对象相同时，可用"that"代替不可数名词或可数名词单数形式，"those"代替可数名词复数形式。本句中"that"指代"the cordiality"，是不可数名词。

例 The books of romance are more popular than those of war among young girls.
在年轻女孩中间，描写浪漫爱情的书比战争的书更受欢迎。

② **They mean nothing but to gratify their own vanity by having an illustrious man in their house.**

这个句子中"but"意为"除了"，常与"nothing/ nobody"连用，表示"就是；不过是"。

例 What he can do is nothing but provide a good place to live for his friends.
他能做的就是给朋友们提供一个好的居所。

经典名句 Famous Classics

1. A Frenchman must be always talking, whether he knows anything of the matter or not; an Englishman is content to say nothing when he has nothing to say. — Samuel Johnson
一个法国人不论其对事情是否有所了解，总是要说；一个英国人当其没啥可说的时候，他甘愿什么也不说。——塞缪尔·约翰逊

2. Not only England, but every Englishman is an island. — Novalis
不但是英国，而且每个英国人都是一个岛。——诺瓦利斯

3. The three wonders of England are the churches, the women and the wool. — Medieval Latin Saying
教堂、女人和羊毛是英国的三大珍品。——中世纪拉丁格言

4. An Englishman thinks he is moral when he is only uncomfortable. — Bernard Shaw
当一个英国人不自在的时候，他便认为自己是有道德的。——萧伯纳

5. With all her faults, she is my country still. — Charles Churchill
她虽有种种缺点，仍然是我的国家。——查理·丘吉尔

6. He who never leaves his country is full of prejudice. — Carlo Goldoni
谁从未离开过本国，谁就偏见最多。——卡罗·戈当里

7. Grief is itself a medicine. — William Cowper, British poet
   悲痛本身也是一种药。——考伯，英国诗人

8. Happiness is beneficial for the body, but it is grief that develops the powers of the mind. — Marcel Proust, French writer
   愉快有益于人的身体，但只有悲伤才能培养心灵力量。——普鲁斯，法国作家

读书笔记

20 Joseph Priestley to His Neighbours of Birmingham
约瑟夫·普利斯特里致邻居伯明翰

London, 19 July 1791

My Late Townsmen and Neighbours,

After living with you eleven years, in which you had uniform experience of my peaceful behaviour, in my attention to the quiet duties of my profession, and those of philosophy, I was far from expecting the injuries which I and my friends have lately received from you. But you have been misled. By hearing the **Dissenters**, and particularly the **Unitarian** Dissenters, continually railed at, as enemies to the present government, in church and state, you have been led to consider any injury done to us a **meritorious** thing; and not having been better informed, the means were not attended to.

When the object was right, you thought the means could not be wrong. By the **discourse** of your teachers, and the exclamations of your superiors in general, drinking confusion and damnation to us (which is well known to have been their frequent practice) your **bigotry** has been excited to the

我曾经的同乡和邻居们：

在和你们生活的11年里，我待人和善，对待工作兢兢业业，一心致力于我的职业和哲学研究，这是大家有目共睹的。可是近来你们对我和我的朋友们造成的伤害是我万万没有料到的。但是，你们大家都被蒙蔽了。由于听信了教会和政府对不信国教者（尤其是唯一神教派信徒）的诋毁，把他们当作政府的敌人，你们就认为伤害我们是一件值得嘉奖的事情。还因为缺乏对事实真相的了解，导致你们采取行动时不择手段。

你们认为目标是对的，手段就不会错。总体上，通过你们老师的长篇大论和上级的激烈言辞，你们被灌输了关于我们的不清楚的观点和对我们的斥责（这是他们众所周知的手段），你们的偏激情绪已经激化到了最高点，而他们不仅不设法缓和反而还在煽风点火。

Joseph Priestley to His Neighbours of Birmingham
约瑟夫·普利斯特里致邻居伯明翰

highest pitch, and nothing having been said to you to **moderate** your passions, but everything to inflame them; hence, without any consideration on your part, or on theirs, who ought to have known, and taught you better, you were prepared for every species of **outrage**; thinking that whatever you could do to spite and injure us, was for the support of government, and especially the church. In destroying us, you have been led to think, you did God and your country the most substantial service.

Happily, the minds of Englishmen have a horror of murder, and therefore you did not, I hope, think of that... but what is the value of life, when everything is done to make it wretched? ...

You have destroyed the most truly valuable and useful **apparatus** of philosophical instruments that perhaps any individual, in this or any other country, was ever possessed of, in my use of which I annually spent large sums, with no **pecuniary** view whatever, but only in the advancement of science, for the benefit of my country and of mankind. You have destroyed a library corresponding to that apparatus, which no money can re-purchase, except in a long course of time. But what I feel far more, you have destroyed manuscripts, which have been the result

因此，无论是你们还是他们，都不再冷静思考（他们本应该知道事情的走向并且本该更好地教导你们），你们准备好了参与任何一场暴行，心想着对我们的所有诅咒和伤害都是对政府的支持，尤其是教会。你们已经被误导了，认为毁灭我们就是你们能为上帝和国家做的最大的功劳。

幸好英国人对杀戮是恐惧的，因此，我希望，你们还没有想过杀人……但如果你们做的一切都是在破坏生命的话，人活着又有什么意义呢？

你们破坏了真正的最价值连城、最有用的东西——我用来研究哲学的仪器——可能是本国或是他国的任何人都不曾拥有过的仪器。我每年都要在这些仪器身上花费大量的金钱，不是为了挣钱，而只是为了科学的进步，为我的国家和整个人类做出贡献。你们毁掉了和仪器配套的书籍资料，这些资料用钱是买不回来的，只能通过时间的积累。但更令我心痛的是，你们烧毁了我的手稿，那是我经年累月、辛苦研究的结果，现在再也不能重新写出来了。而这一切都降临在一个从来没有伤害过或想过要伤害你们的人身上……

of the **laborious** study of many years, and which I shall never be able to re-compose; and this has been done to one who never did, or imagined, you any harm...

You are still more mistaken, if you imagine that this conduct of yours has any tendency to serve your cause, or to prejudice ours. It is nothing but reason and argument that can ever support any system of religion. Answer our arguments, and your business is done; but your having **recourse** to violence, is only a proof that you have nothing better to produce. Should you destroy myself, as well as my house, library, and apparatus, ten more persons, of equal or superior spirit and ability, would instantly rise up. If those ten were destroyed, an hundred would appear...

...In this business we are the sheep and you the wolves. We will preserve our character, and hope you will change yours. **At all events**, we return you blessings for curses; and pray that you may soon return to that industry, and those sober manners, for which the inhabitants of Birmingham were formerly distinguished.

    I am, your sincere well-wisher,
        J. Priestley

你们要是觉得这样做对你们的事业有任何好处,或是对我们的事业有任何损害,那就大错特错了。能够支撑任何一个宗教体系的无非是理智和论辩。回应我们提出的论点,你们的任务就完成了;但诉诸武力恰恰证明你们对此无力回击。如果你们像烧毁我的房屋、藏书室和仪器一样毁灭我的话,立刻会有10个在精神和才学上和我一样或高我一等的人站出来。如果你们把这10个人也毁灭掉,那么会有100个人站出来……

……在这样的斗争中,我们是羔羊,你们是豺狼。我们的本性不会变,希望你们的能够改变。无论如何,我们要用祝福来回应诅咒。我们祈祷,你们很快能回到和伯明翰先人一样特有的冷静审慎的举止和勤奋刻苦的态度。

衷心祝愿你们的
约瑟夫·普利斯特里
1791年7月19日于伦敦

Joseph Priestley to His Neighbours of Birmingham
约瑟夫·普利斯特里致邻居伯明翰

单词解析 Word Analysis

dissenter [dɪˈsentə(r)] *n.* 持异议者；不信奉英国国教的英国新教徒

例 The Party does not tolerate dissenters in its ranks.
该政党不允许其成员中存在异议分子。

unitarian [ˌjuːnɪˈteərɪən] *adj.* 唯一神派的

例 The spirits of American sustained his exploitation in all realms, and the belief in Unitarian inspired his service to the common.
美国精神支持他不断在各领域开拓，唯一神论信仰激励他服务大众的决心。

meritorious [ˌmerɪˈtɔːrɪəs] *adj.* 值得称赞的

例 Perform meritorious service to atone for one's crimes so as to obtain clemency from the people.
立功赎罪，以求得人民的宽恕。

discourse [ˈdɪskɔːs] *n.* 论述，交谈

例 Gates responds with a lengthy discourse on deployment strategy.
盖茨以一篇有关部署策略的鸿篇大论予以回应。

bigotry [ˈbɪɡətri] *n.* 盲从；偏执

例 One of the important features of terrorism is the fanaticism and bigotry in thinking.
恐怖主义的一个重要特征就是思想的狂热与偏执。

moderate [ˈmɒdərət] *vt.* 使和缓

例 They are hoping that once in office he can be persuaded to moderate his views.
他们希望等他一上台，可以说服他观点别那么激进。

outrage [ˈaʊtreɪdʒ] *n.* 暴行；骇人听闻的事

例 The latest outrage was to have been a coordinated gun and bomb attack on the station.
最近的一起暴行是同时动用了枪支和炸弹的对车站的袭击。

apparatus [ˌæpəˈreɪtəs] *n.* 仪器，器械

例 The apparatus is spotlessly clean.

仪器上一尘不染。

pecuniary [pɪˈkjuːniəri] *adj.* 金钱的，金钱上的

例 She denies obtaining a pecuniary advantage by deception.
她否认通过欺骗手段获得经济利益。

laborious [ləˈbɔːriəs] *adj.* 费力的；辛苦的

例 Keeping the garden tidy all year round can be a laborious task.
一年到头把花园拾掇得干净整洁也不是件轻松活儿。

recourse [rɪˈkɔːs] *n.* 依靠；依赖；求助

例 It enabled its members to settle their differences without recourse to war.
这样，其成员就可以不必诉诸战争来解决分歧。

at all events 不管发生什么事，在任何情况下，无论如何

例 At all events, it's better to try than sit around doing nothing.
无论怎样，去尝试总比坐在那里无所事事要好。

语法知识点 Grammar Points

① After living with you eleven years, in which you had uniform experience of my peaceful behaviour, in my attention to the quiet duties of my profession, and those of philosophy, I was far from expecting the injuries which I and my friends have lately received from you.

这个句子中"after"引导一个时间状语从句，从句省略了主语"I"。由于从句主语和主句主语一致，所以可以省略，并且从句中的动词跟在"after"后用现在分词形式。

例 After being fired, he became rather depressed and spiritless.
被解雇后，他变得十分消沉沮丧。

② It is nothing but reason and argument that can ever support any system of religion.

这个句子中用到了"it is... that..."的句型，突出强调"is"后的部分。

例 It is my mom that sacrifices the most for my family.
我的母亲才是为家庭牺牲最大的人。

③ **Should you destroy myself, as well as my house, library, and apparatus, ten more persons, of equal or superior spirit and ability, would instantly rise up.**

这个句子中用到了"if"引导的带有虚拟语气的条件状语从句，从句中"should/ had/ were"可提前，并省略"if"。

例 Should the weather be fine tomorrow, we could go and have a picnic.
要是明天天气好的话，我们就可以去野餐。

经典名句 Famous Classics

1. One knows even when one neighbour's bread is in the oven. — Ghanaian Proverb
一个人甚至可以知道邻居的面包是不是在烤箱里。——加纳谚语

2. Our neighbour's children are always the worst. — German Proverb
邻居的孩子总是最差的。——德国谚语

3. We make our friends; we make our enemies, but God makes our next-door neighbour. — G. K. Chesterton
朋友是我们自己选择的，敌人是我们自己树立的，但是隔壁的邻居是上帝安排的。——G. K. 切斯特顿

4. All men are moral. Only their neighbours are not. — John Steinbeck
所有人都是道德的，除了他们的邻居。——斯坦贝克

5. In our efforts to adjust differences of opinion we should be free from intolerance of passion, and our judgements should be unmoved by alluring phrases and unvexed by selfish interests. — Grover Cleveland
在我们努力协调意见的分歧时，应当抛弃偏执与意气用事；我们的判断不应当被花言巧语蒙骗，也不应被个人私利扰乱。——克利夫兰，美国总统

6. Love your neighbour, yet pull not down your hedge. — English Proverb
爱你的左邻右舍，但不要拆去你们之间的藩篱。——英国谚语

7. Permanent good can never be the outcome of untruth and violence. — Gandhi
通过虚假和暴力不会得到永恒的善。——甘地

8. Science has no room for racism. — Nelson Mandela
科学不分种族。——纳尔逊·曼德拉

读书笔记

21 Thomas Jefferson to Giovanni Fabbroni
托马斯·杰斐逊致吉奥凡尼·法布罗尼

Williamsburg in Virginia, June 8, 1778

...If there is a gratification which I envy any people in this world it is to your country its music. This is the favorite passion of my soul, and fortune has cast my lot in a country where it is in a state of **deplorable barbarism**. From the line of life in which we **conjecture** you to be, I have for some time lost the hope of seeing you here. Should the event prove so, I shall ask your assistance in procuring a substitute, who may be a proficient in singing, and on the harpsichord. I should be contented to receive such one two or three years hence, when it is hoped he may come more safely, and find here a greater plenty of those useful things which commerce alone can **furnish**.

The bounds of an American fortune will not admit the indulgence of a domestic band of musicians. Yet I have thought that a passion for music might be reconciled with that economy which we are obliged to observe. I retain for instance among my domestic servants

……如果这个世界上有一种令人满意和喜悦的事物让我羡慕它的民族的话，那么非贵国的音乐莫属。音乐是我内心的挚爱，但是命运把我降生在一个音乐极不成熟的国家。根据我们对您生活轨迹的猜测，我早已不抱希望能在这里见到您了。如果真是这样的话，我希望您能帮我物色一个能替代您来美国的擅长歌唱与弹琴的音乐家。如果今后的两三年内能有合适的人选，我就已经很满足了，希望到那时他能更安全地抵达美国，并且能在这里发现更多有用的东西，而这些东西是只有商业可以提供的。

一个美国人的财力是不足以支撑一个家庭乐队的。然而我认为对音乐的喜爱必须与财力相协调。比如，我在我的家仆中保留了一个园丁、一个纺织工、一个细木工和一个石工，还有意再雇一名葡萄种植工人。在像意大利这样的国家

a gardener (Ortolano), a weaver (Tessitore di lino e lano), a cabinet maker (Stipettaio) and a stonecutter (Scalpellino lavorante in piano) to which I would add a vigneron. In a country where, like yours, music is cultivated and practiced by every class of men I suppose there might be found persons of those trades who could perform on the French horn, clarinet or hautboy and bassoon, so that one might have a band of two French horns, two clarinets, and hautboys and a bassoon, without enlarging their domestic expenses. A certainty of employment for a half dozen years, and at the end of that time to find them if they choose a **conveyance** to their own country might **induce** them to come here on reasonable wages. Without meaning to give you trouble, perhaps it might be practicable for you in your ordinary intercourse with your people to find out such men **disposed** to come to America. **Sobriety** and good nature would be desirable parts of their characters. If you think such a plan practicable, and will be so kind as to inform me what will be necessary expenses, when informed of them, I can **remit** before they are wanting, to any port in France with which country alone we have safe correspondence.

  I am Sir with much esteem your humble servant.

里，人人都学习和演奏音乐，我想贵国从事上述职业的人中也可能有会吹法国圆号、单簧管、高音双簧管和低音管的，这样一来，组建一支有两个圆号演奏者、两个单簧管演奏者、两个高音双簧管演奏者和一个低音管演奏者的乐队也是有可能的，也不会增加家里的开销。雇用期定为六年，期满之后，如果他们想要回国，我一定送他们回去，这两个条件再加上合理的工资，也许能够吸引他们来这里。我无意给您添麻烦，您只需要在平常和人聊天时问一下有没有人愿意来美国。他们最好头脑清醒，脾气温和。如果您觉得这个计划是可行的，并且十分好意地告知有任何必要的花销后，我会立即寄往法国——我们唯一能安全通信的国家——的任何一个港口。

您谦恭的仆人向先生您致以敬意
1778年6月8日于弗吉尼亚州威廉斯堡

Thomas Jefferson to Giovanni Fabbroni
托马斯·杰斐逊致吉奥凡尼·法布罗尼

单词解析 Word Analysis

deplorable [dɪˈplɔːrəbl] *adj.* 糟透的，可叹的

> Many of them live under deplorable conditions.
> 他们中很多人的生活条件极其恶劣。

barbarism [ˈbɑːbərɪzəm] *n.* 野蛮；未开化

> We do not ask for the death penalty: barbarism must not be met with barbarism.
> 我们不赞成死刑：不能以暴制暴。

conjecture [kənˈdʒektʃə(r)] *v.* 猜测；推测

> We can only conjecture about what was in the killer's mind.
> 我们只能猜测当时凶手心里想的是什么。

furnish [ˈfɜːnɪʃ] *v.* 向（某人/某事物）供应，提供

> They'll be able to furnish you with the rest of the details.
> 他们将向你提供其余的细节。

conveyance [kənˈveɪəns] *n.* 运送；传送；运输工具

> Mahoney had never seen such a conveyance before.
> 马奥尼以前从来没有见过这样的运输工具。

induce [ɪnˈdjuːs] *vt.* 劝说；诱使

> Music can induce a meditative state in the listener.
> 音乐能够引导倾听者沉思。

disposed [dɪˈspəʊzd] *adj.* 倾向于；有意于

> We passed one or two dwellings, but were not disposed to stop.
> 我们路过了一两个歇脚处，但却无意驻足。

sobriety [səˈbraɪəti] *n.* 清醒；节制

> You had to speak to Henry in those moments of sobriety.
> 你必须在亨利清醒的时刻同他讲话。

remit [ˈriːmɪt] *v.* 汇（款）；寄（钱）

> Many immigrants regularly remit money to their families.

许多移民定期给他们的家人汇款。

语法知识点 *Grammar Points*

① This is the favorite passion of my soul, and fortune has cast my lot in a country where it is in a state of deplorable barbarism.

这个句子中有一个"where"引导的定语从句,先行词为"country"。定语从句的先行词为表示地点的名词,且在从句中做地点状语时,关系副词用"where"。

例 We are planning to travel to Italy where my husband and I had honeymoon.
我们打算去意大利旅游,我和我丈夫的蜜月就是在那儿度过的。

② Should the event prove so, I shall ask your assistance in procuring a substitute, who may be a proficient in singing, and on the harpsichord.

这个句子中"should the event prove so"是一个含有虚拟语气的条件状语从句,句中"if"被省略,且"should"被前置至句首。"if"引导的含有虚拟语气的条件句中,如果从句中含有"had/should/were"时,可将这三个词提前并省略"if"。

例 Were we adults, we would be able to change the world.
如果我们是大人的话,就能改变世界了。

③ If you think such a plan practicable, and will be so kind as to inform me what will be necessary expenses, when informed of them, I can remit before they are wanting, to any port in France with which country alone we have safe correspondence.

这个句子中有一个"when"引导的时间状语从句,句中省略了主语和谓语动词,即"I"和"am"。当"when"引导的时间状语从句的主语和主句主语一致,并且谓语动词为"be"时,从句的主语和谓语动词均可省略。

例 When told the news that his wife was missing, he was thrown into great sorrow.
当被告知妻子失踪时,他陷入极大的痛苦当中。

Thomas Jefferson to Giovanni Fabbroni
托马斯·杰斐逊致吉奥凡尼·法布罗尼

经典名句 Famous Classics

1. Without music, life would be a mistake. — Friedrich Nietzsche
   没有音乐，生活将是一个错误。——弗里德里希·尼采

2. Music is the medicine of a troubled mind. — Walter Haddon
   音乐是治疗心灵苦恼的药。——沃尔特·哈登

3. The history of a country is written in its popular songs. — Unknown
   一个国家的历史写在它的民歌之中。——佚名

4. Music is an indication to love. — Latin Proverb
   音乐是一种爱的表露。——拉丁谚语

5. Music is the art of thinking with sounds. — Jules Combarieu
   音乐是用声音思考的艺术。——J. 孔巴略

6. Anything too stupid to be said, is sung. — Voltaire
   说出来愚蠢的话唱出来就不一样了。——伏尔泰

7. I am not afraid of tomorrow for I have seen yesterday and I love today. — Thomas Jefferson
   我不缅怀过去的历史，而致力于未来的梦想。——托马斯·杰斐逊

8. Music with dinner is an insult both to the cook and the violinist. — G. K. Chesterton
   吃饭时的音乐对厨师和小提琴手都是一种侮辱。——G. K. 切斯特顿

22 Thomas Jefferson to Martha Jefferson
托马斯·杰斐逊致玛莎·杰斐逊

Annapolis, November 28, 1783

My Dear Patsy,

After four days journey I arrived here without any accident and in as good health as when I left Philadelphia. The **conviction** that you would be more improved in the situation I have placed you than if still with me, has **solaced** me on my parting with you, which my love for you has rendered a difficult thing. The **acquirements** which I hope you will make under the tutors I have provided for you will **render** you more worthy of my love, and if they cannot increase it they will prevent its **diminution**. Consider the good lady who has taken you under her roof, who has undertaken to see that you perform all your exercises, and to **admonish** you in all those wanderings from what is right or what is clever to which your inexperience would expose you; consider her I say as your mother, as the only person to whom, since the loss with which heaven has been pleased to afflict you, you can now look up; and that her

我亲爱的帕齐:

经过四天的旅程,我平安到达了这里,身体也和离开费城时一样好。我深信,和仍然与我在一起相比,在我为你做的安排下,你能生活得更好,这样想能让我在离开时不那么伤心。我对你的爱使得我们的分离并非易事。我为你请了一些老师,在他们的教导下,我希望你能取得进步,这样你才值得我这么爱你,就算这一切没有什么效果,至少也不会对你有损。要尊重这位收留你的善良的夫人,她负责监督你完成任务,负责在你由于缺乏经验而偏离正确明智的道路时给出建议和劝导。你要把她当作母亲来看待,在上天使你不幸遭受丧母之痛后,她就是你唯一能仰仗的人了。任何时候你要是莽莽撞撞地惹她不开心或是不满意了,将会是一笔巨大的损失,要想重归于好可就难了。至于你的时间分配问题,

Thomas Jefferson to Martha Jefferson

托马斯·杰斐逊致玛莎·杰斐逊

displeasure or **disapprobation** on any occasion will be an immense misfortune which should you be so unhappy as to incur by any unguarded act, think no concession too much to regain her good will. With respect to the distribution of your time the following is what I should approve.

From 8 to 10 o'clock practise music

From 10 to 1 dance one day and draw another

From 1 to 2 draw on the day you dance, and write a letter the next day

From 3 to 4 read French

From 4 to 5 exercise yourself in music

From 5 till bedtime read English, write English.

Communicate this plan to Mrs. Hopkinson and if she approves of it pursue it. As long as Mrs. Trist remains in Philadelphia cultivate her affections. She has been a valuable friend to you and her good sense and good heart make her valued by all who know her and by nobody on earth more than by me. I expect you will write to me by every post. Inform me what books you read, what tunes you learn, and inclose me your best copy of every lesson in drawing. Write also one letter every week either to your aunt Eppes, your aunt Skipwith, your aunt Carr, or the

我认为如下的安排是可行的：

上午8点至10点：学习音乐

上午10点至下午1点：学习舞蹈以及画画（隔天进行）

下午1点至2点：画画和写信（隔天进行，学舞蹈的那天下午就画画）

下午3点至4点：读法语

下午4点至5点：练习音乐

下午5点至睡觉前：读写英语

告诉霍普金森夫人这个安排，如果她同意的话，就这样执行。只要特里斯特女士还在费城，你要和她培养感情。她对你而言是一个珍贵的朋友。她既有远见卓识，又心地善良，认识她的人都十分看重她。我也是如此，这个世界上估计没有人比我更看重她了。每次邮差来送信的时候，我都期待有你的来信。告诉我你读了什么书、学了什么曲子，把绘画课上画的最好的一张附寄给我。还要每周写一封信，给埃普斯姨妈、斯基普威思姨妈、卡尔姨妈或是我正在回信的这位小女士。每次给我写信时也要附上一份你给她们写的信。要留心不要犯拼写错误。每次下笔写一个词之前，要想好它是怎么拼写的，如果不记得它的拼写，那就查字典。一

little lady from whom I now **inclose** a letter, and always put the letter you so write **under cover to** me. Take care that you never spell a wrong word. Always before you write a word consider how it is spelt, and if you do not remember it, turn to a dictionary. It produces a great praise to a lady to spell well. I have placed my happiness on seeing you good and accomplished, and no distress which this world can now bring on me could equal that of your disappointing my hopes. If you love me then, strive to be good under every situation and to all living creatures, and to acquire those accomplishments which I have put in your power, and which will go far towards ensuring you the warmest love of your affectionate father.

P. S. Keep my letters and read them at times that you may always have present in your mind those things which will endear you to me.

位不犯拼写错误的淑女是非常受人称赞的。我全部的幸福就是看到你品德良好、有所成就，在这个世界上，没有什么比你辜负我的期望更令我痛苦了。如果你爱我的话，就要努力在任何时候都保持品德，善良地对待一切生物，并且取得我所期望的成就，这样你才能确保我最温暖的爱。

另：保存好我的信件，不时翻阅，以便铭记那些父女之间的温情时刻。

1783年11月28日于安纳波利斯

单词解析 Word Analysis

conviction [kən'vɪkʃn] *n.* 信念，深信

例 Their religious convictions prevented them from taking up arms.
由于宗教信仰的原因，他们不会拿起武器进行反抗。

solace ['sɒləs] *vt.* 安慰，慰藉

例 His way of solacing himself is just sleeping.
他宽慰自己的方式就是睡觉。

acquirement [ə'kwaɪəmənt] *n.* 取得，习得

例 The language acquirement usually happens more effectively in childhood.
通常，童年时语言的习得更有效。

render ['rendə(r)] *n.* 使成为；使变得

例 Hundreds of people were rendered homeless by the earthquake.
成百上千的人因为地震而无家可归。

diminution [ˌdɪmɪ'njuːʃn] *n.* 减小，减少

例 The president has accepted a diminution of the powers he originally wanted.
总统已经接受了对自己原本要求的权力进行削减。

admonish [əd'mɒnɪʃ] *vt.* 劝告；训诫

例 The ethics committee may take a decision to admonish him or to censure him.
道德委员会也许会决定对他进行训诫或是严厉批评。

disapprobation [ˌdɪsˌæprə'beɪʃn] *n.* 不同意，不满

例 The candidate was interrupted in a speech by clamors of disapprobation.
这位候选人的演说因反对的叫嚣声而中断。

inclose [ɪn'kləʊz] *vt.* 附上

例 Please inclose us a recent photo of yourself with your resume.
请随简历附上一张本人的近照。

under cover to *adv.* 附在信中

例 This letter is addressed to him under cover to his friend.
这封信是附在给他朋友的信内寄给他的。

语法知识点 Grammar Points

① **After four days journey I arrived here without any accident and in as good health as when I left Philadelphia.**

这个句子中"as good health as when I left Philadelphia"是一个同级比较结构，将现在的情况与"when I left Philadelphia"做比较，比较的对象为"health"，第一个"as"后只能接形容词或副词，表示程度。

例 My hometown has as many mountains as yours.
我家乡的山和你家乡的一样多。

② **She has been a valuable friend to you and her good sense and good heart make her valued by all who know her and by nobody on earth more than by me.**

这个句子中"make her valued"是"使役动词+宾语+过去分词"的用法，表示"使某人/某事被……"。

例 When talking with others, you need to speak in a proper volume and speed so as to make yourself understood.
当和别人交谈时，你应该保持合适的音量和语速以使别人能够听懂。

③ **I have placed my happiness on seeing you good and accomplished, and no distress which this world can now bring on me could equal that of your disappointing my hopes.**

这个句子中"that"为代词，指代"distress"，常用于比较级中，替代前文提到的比较对象。如果比较对象为复数，则用"those"。

例 The weather here is much hotter than that in my hometown.
这里的天气比我的家乡要热得多。

经典名句 Famous Classics

1. One father is more than a hundred schoolmasters. — English Proverb
1个爸爸比100个校长还顶用。——英国谚语

2. The most important thing a father can do for his children is to love their mother. — Theodore Hesburgh

Thomas Jefferson to Martha Jefferson
托马斯·杰斐逊致玛莎·杰斐逊

一个父亲能为子女做的最重要的事情就是爱他们的母亲。——西奥多·赫斯伯格

3. It is a wise father that knows his own child. — William Shakespeare
   父贤知其子。——威廉·莎士比亚

4. I cannot think of any need in childhood as strong as the need for a father's protection. — Sigmund Freud
   我想不到童年时除了需要父亲的保护还需要什么。——弗洛伊德

5. When a father gives to his son, both laugh; when a son gives to his father, both cry. — Jewish Proverb
   当父亲给予孩子时,两人都无比开心。而当孩子回报父亲时,两人皆泪流满面。——犹太谚语

6. It is not flesh and blood, but heart which makes us fathers and sons. — Friedrich von Schiller
   父子不仅血肉至亲,更是灵魂相依。——弗里德里希·冯·席勒

7. I am blessed to be a proud father of a daughter. — Adnan Sami
   我很荣幸有一个让我骄傲的女儿。——阿德南·萨米,印度歌手

8. I love my mother and father. The older I get, the more I value everything that they gave me. — Liev Schreiber
   我爱我的父母,越长大,我越珍惜他们给我的一切。——列维·施瑞博尔,美国演员

读书笔记

23 Robert Southey to Charlotte Brontë
罗伯特·骚塞致夏洛特·勃朗蒂

Keswick, March, 1837

Madam,

You will probably, **ere** this, have given up all expectation of receiving an answer to your letter of December 29. I was on the borders of Cornwall when the letter was written; it found me a fortnight afterwards in Hampshire. During my subsequent movements in different parts of the country, and a **tarriance** of three busy weeks in London, I had no leisure for replying to it; and now that I am once more at home, and am **clearing off** the **arrears** of business which have accumulated during a long absence, it has lain unanswered till the last of a numerous life, not from disrespect or indifference to its contents, but because, in truth, it is not an easy task to answer it, nor a pleasant one to cast a damp over the high spirits and the generous desires of youth.

What you are I can only infer from your letter, which appears to be written in sincerity, though I may suspect that you have used a **fictitious** signature.

女士：

可能在收到这封信之前，你已经不奢望我能回复你12月29日写给我的那封信了吧。你写信的时候我正在康沃尔郡的边境，两周后，我才在汉普郡收到此信。后来我一直在全国各地奔波，又在伦敦耽误了三个礼拜，我太忙了以至于没有闲暇来回信。现在我又回到了家，清理由于长期在外而积压的未尽事宜。直到处理完一大批文件后，我才开始给你回信，这不是因为我不尊重或者不关心你来信的内容，事实上是因为这封信回复起来并没那么容易，我也不愿意给兴致高涨、野心勃勃的年轻人泼冷水。

你的来信看起来是真心写就的，尽管我怀疑你用了假名，我只能从信中推测你的为人了。无论怎样，你的信和诗有相同的风格，我也能很好地理解它们传达的思想。我是怎样的人，你可能已经从手中那

Robert Southey to Charlotte Brontë
罗伯特·骚塞致夏洛特·勃朗蒂

Be that as it may, the letter and the verse **bear the same stamp**; and I can well understand the state of mind they indicate. What I am you might have learnt by such of my publications as have come into your hands; and had you happened to be acquainted with me, a little personal knowledge would have tempered your enthusiasm. You might have had your ardour in some degree abated by seeing a poet in the decline of life, and witnessing the effect which age produces upon our hopes and aspirations; yet I am neither a disappointed man nor a discontented one, and you would never have heard from me any chilling **sermons** upon the text "All is Vanity".

It is not my advice that you have asked as to the direction of your talents, but my opinion of them; and yet the opinion may be worth little, and the advice much. You evidently possesses, and in no inconsiderable degree, what Wordsworth calls the "faculty of verse". I am not **depreciating** it when I say that in these times it is not rare. Many volumes of poets are now published every year without attracting public attention, anyone of which, if it had appeared half a century ago, would have obtained a high reputation for its author. Whoever, therefore, is ambitious

些我发表的著作中得知了。假如你碰巧认识我，对我个人的了解可能会冲淡你的热情。因为见到一个迟暮的诗人，见到岁月对人的希望和抱负做出的改变，你的热情在某种程度上会有所降低。然而我既不灰心丧气，也不贪得无厌，从我这里你永远不会听到"凡事皆是虚空"这样的说教。

至于你该朝哪个方向施展才华，你向我询问的是看法而不是建议。但是，我的看法远不如建议那么重要。很明显，你拥有华兹华斯所称的"诗才"，而且不少。当我说这样的诗才如今并不少见时，我没有贬低它的意思。如今每年都有很多诗集出版，但是大众的关注度却不高。这其中的任何一本，放在半个世纪以前，都会给作者带来极高的声誉。因此，要是有人想以这种方式出名的话，要做好失望的打算。

但是如果你为了自己的幸福着想的话，就不应该为了出名而培养这项才能。文学是我终身追求的职业，尽管我从没有为这一慎重思考后的选择后悔过，我还是认为自己有责任劝诫满怀抱负地向我求取鼓励与建议的后辈不要从事这一危险的职业。你会说女人不需要

of distinction in this way ought to be prepared for disappointment.

But it is not with a view to distinction that you should cultivate this talent, if you consult your own happiness. I, who have made literature my profession, and devoted my life to it, and have never for a moment repented of the deliberate choice, think myself, nevertheless, bound in duty to caution every young man who applies as an **aspirant** to me for encouragement and advice against taking so **perilous** a course. You will say that a woman has no need of such a caution; there can be no peril in it for her. In a certain sense this is true; but there is a danger of which I would, with all kindness and all earnestness, warn you. The day dreams in which you habitually indulge are likely to induce a **distempered** state of mind; and, in proportion as all the ordinary uses of the world seem to you flat and unprofitable, you will be unfitted for them without becoming fitted for anything else. Literature cannot be the business of a woman's life, and it ought not to be. The more she is engaged in her proper duties, the less leisure will she have for it, even as an **accomplishment** and a recreation. To those duties you have yet not been called, and when you are you will be less eager for celebrity. You will

这样的劝诫，文学对她没有危险。在某种意义上，这是正确的；但是有一种危险，我必须带着全部的善意和恳切来警告你。你深陷其中的白日梦很可能带来思维的混乱。在你把世间的一切职业都看得平淡无奇和毫无价值可言时，你也就不适应这些工作了，最终一事无成。文学不可能也不应该作为女性的终身职业。她要履行的日常职责越多，她可以写作的闲暇时间就越少，即使只是作为一种技艺或者消遣。你还没有被要求履行那些职责，一旦需要履行，你就不会那么渴望成名了。你将不必从想象中寻求刺激，因为不论你处于怎样的境况之中，生活的起起伏伏和无法逃脱的焦虑都会给你带来太多的刺激。

但是不要认为我轻视你的才华，我也不会阻止你施展它。我这样劝导你只是为了让你再三思考怎样运用自己的才华以使自己终身受益。要单纯地为了诗歌而写诗，不要想着与人攀比或是出人头地。你越不急功近利，你越能配得上享有名声，最后也越有可能获得名声。这样写作对身心都是有益的。这可能是除宗教之外最能宽慰心灵、提升精神境界的方法了。你可以在诗中包

not seek in imagination for excitement, of which the **vicissitudes** of the life, and the anxieties from which you must not hope to be exempted, be your state what it may, will bring with them but too much.

But do not suppose that I **disparage** the gift which you possess, nor that I would discourage you from exercising it, as to render it conducive to your own permanent good. Write poetry for its own sake; not in a spirit of emulation, and not with a view to celebrity; the less you aim at that the more likely you will be to deserve and finally to obtain it. So written, it is **wholesome** both for the heart and soul; it may be made the surest means, next to religion, of soothing the mind, and elevating it. You may embody in it your best thoughts and your wisest feelings, and in so doing discipline and strengthening them.

Farewell, madam. It is not because I have forgotten that I was once young myself, that I write to you in this **strain**; but because I remember it. You will neither doubt my sincerity, nor my goodwill; and however ill what has here been said may accord with your present views and temper, the longer you live the more reasonable it will appear to you. Though I may be an **ungracious** adviser, you will allow me, therefore, to

涵最好的想法和最敏锐的情感，这样也可以使它们得到训练和强化。

再见，女士。我以这样的口吻给你写信，不是因为我忘记了自己的年轻时光，而是因为我记得。你无须怀疑我的真诚和好意。不论我说的有多不符合你现在的观点和性情，你活得越久，越会发现这是忠言逆耳。我可能不是一个让人愉快的劝告者，但仍然希望你能允许我以如下方式落款，祝你永远幸福。——你真心的朋友，

罗伯特·骚塞
1837年3月于凯斯维克

subscribe myself, with the best wishes for your happiness here and hereafter, your true friend,

Robert Southey

单词解析 Word Analysis

ere [eə(r)] *prep.* 在……之前

> It was not long ere a call came from the house and recalled me from my reflections.
> 不久，家里打来了电话，把我从沉思中唤醒。

tarriance ['tærɪəns] *n.* 拖延，耽搁

> After having finished the service in Yorkshire, I have had a week's tarriance at Harrowgate.
> 在约克郡服役期满后，我在哈罗盖特耽搁了一周时间。

clear off 清算，完成

> The mall decided to clear off the summer clothes when the new winter fashions arrived.
> 那家商场购进新的冬季时装时，决定把夏季服装廉价处理掉。

arrears [ə'rɪəz] *n.* 逾期欠款，未完成的事

> They have promised to pay the arrears over the next five years.
> 他们保证在随后的5年内偿付逾期债款。

fictitious [fɪk'tɪʃəs] *adj.* 虚构的；虚假的

> The story my mother told me when I was young is fictitious.
> 小时候妈妈对我讲的那个故事是虚构的。

bear the stamp 带有……风格

> Their tactics bear the stamp of Soviet military training.
> 他们的战术带有苏联军事训练的印记。

sermon ['sɜːmən] *n.* 布道；讲道

> At High Mass the priest preached a sermon on the devil.

牧师在大弥撒上布道驱邪。

depreciate [dɪˈpriːʃieɪt] *vt.* 贬低；轻视

例 All the works of man have their origin in creative fantasy. What right have we then to depreciate imagination?
人类的所有成就都源于创造性幻想。那么我们有什么权利轻视想象力呢？

aspirant [əˈspaɪərənt] *n.* 有志向或渴望获得……的人

例 He is among the few aspirants with administrative experience.
他是为数不多的几个志向远大而且有管理经验的人之一。

perilous [ˈperələs] *adj.* 危险的，冒险的

例 The road grew even steeper and more perilous.
道路变得越来越陡峭，越来越凶险。

distempered [dɪsˈtempəd] *adj.* 不健全的，紊乱的

例 Distempered Personality leads to his tragedy.
病态的性格导致了他悲剧的命运。

accomplishment [əˈkʌmplɪʃmənt] *n.* 才艺；技艺；专长

例 She is fond of learning new accomplishments.
她很喜欢学习新才艺。

vicissitude [vɪˈsɪsɪtjuːd] *n.* 变迁；人生的沉浮

例 So great a vicissitude in her life could not at once be received as real.
她的生活中发生了如此巨大的变迁，她一时还无法相信是真的。

disparage [dɪˈspærɪdʒ] *vt.* 贬低；轻视

例 The tax cut is widely disparaged by senators from both parties as a budget gimmick.
两个党派的参议员们普遍对作为预算噱头的税收削减嗤之以鼻。

exhort [ɪgˈzɔːt] *v.* 规劝；敦促

例 Kennedy exhorted his listeners to turn away from violence.
肯尼迪劝诫听众远离暴力。

wholesome ['həulsəm] *adj.* 有益健康的；有益身心的

例 My mood this year is for a cosy, nice and thoroughly wholesome Christmas.
我今年想过一个温馨、愉快并且绝对健康的圣诞节。

strain [streɪn] *n.* 气质；特性；风格；作风

例 There was a strain of bitterness in his voice.
他的声音听起来有些愤愤不平。

ungracious [ʌnˈgreɪʃəs] *adj.* 不客气的，失礼的

例 It would be most ungracious and impolite to refuse a simple invitation to supper with him.
连与他共进晚餐这样的简单邀请都拒绝会显得非常失礼，没有教养。

语法知识点 Grammar Points

① **Be that as it may, the letter and the verse bear the same stamp; and I can well understand the state of mind they indicate.**

这个句子中"be that as it may"是由"as"引导的让步状语从句，原句语序应为"as it may be that"。"as"引导的让步状语从句通常置于句首，并将实义动词、形容词、副词、名词提前。

例 Try as he might, he failed again.
尽管他尝试了，他还是失败了。

② **It is not my advice that you have asked as to the direction of your talents, but my opinion of them.**

这个句子是强调句句型，强调"not my advice but my opinion of them"，去掉"it is... that..."后句子应为"as to the direction of your talents, you have asked not my advice but my opinion of them"。其中"not... but..."表示"不是……而是……"。

例 It is not the book but the author that is to blame for its bad effects on teenagers.
是作者而不是书应该因对青少年的不良影响而受谴责。

③ **The more she is engaged in her proper duties, the less leisure will she have for it, even as an accomplishment and a recreation.**

这个句子是"the + 比较级，the + 比较级"的句型，意为"越……，越……"。

例 The more you envy others, the less you will be satisfied with what you have had.

你越羡慕别人，越会对自己拥有的感到不满足。

经典名句 Famous Classics

1. There are two powers in the world; one is the sword and the other is the pen. There is a great competition and rivalry between the two. There is a third power stronger than both, that of the women. — Muhmamad Ali Jinah

   世界上最强大的两种东西，一种是剑，一种是笔。这两者之间有很大的竞争性。世界上还有比这两种东西更强大的第三种，那就是女人。——穆罕默德·阿里·吉娜

2. Women will never be as successful as men because they have no wives to advise them. — Dick Van Dyke

   女性绝不会有和男人一样的成功，因为她们没有妻子给她们建议。——迪克·范·戴克

3. Girls have an unfair advantage over men: if they can't get what they want by being smart, they can get it by being dumb. — Yul Brynner

   女孩儿有男孩儿没有的优势：如果她们不能通过变聪明得到她们想要的，那么她们可以通过变得愚笨得到。——尤尔·伯连纳

4. Being a woman is a terribly difficult task, since it consists principally in dealing with men. — Joseph Conrad

   做女人难，因为主要是和男人打交道。——约瑟夫·康拉德

5. Women are like tea bags; put them in hot water and they get stronger. — Eleanor Roosevelt

   女人就像茶包，在热水中变得更加浓烈。——埃莉诺·罗斯福

6. Life of reaction is a life of slavery, intellectually and spiritually. One must fight for a life of action, not reaction. —Rita Mae Brown, Feminist
在事情发生才做反应的人生，是一个奴役的人生，无论以心灵或智能层面来讲。我们要为一个主动，而非被动的人生奋斗。——丽塔·梅·布朗（女权主义者）

7. I am poor, humble, not beautiful, but when our souls through the grave came to god, we are all equal. — *Jane Eyre*
我贫穷，卑微，不美丽，但当我们的灵魂穿过坟墓来到上帝面前时，我们都是平等的。——《简·爱》

8. It is easier to live through someone else than to become complete yourself. — Betty Friedan, Feminist
以别人的方式生活，比完全成为你自己还要容易。——贝蒂·傅瑞丹（女权主义者）

读书笔记

24 Charles Lamb to S. T. Coleridge
查尔斯·兰姆致塞·泰·柯勒律治

24 October 1796

Coleridge,

I feel myself much your **debtor** for that spirit of confidence and friendship which dictated your last letter. May your soul find peace at last in your cottage life! I only wish you were but settled. Do continue to write to me. I read your let ers with my sister, and they give us both abundance of delight. Especially they please us two, when you talk in a religious strain, —not but we are offended occasionally with a certain freedom of expression, a certain **air** of mysticism, more **consonant** to the **conceits** of **pagan** philosophy, than consistent with the **humility** of genuine piety. For instance now in your last letter –you say, 'It is by the press, that God hath given finite spirits both evil and good (I suppose you mean simply bad men and good men) a portion of it were of His **Omnipresence**!' Now, high as the human intellect comparatively will soar, and wide as its influence, malign or salutary, can extend, is there

柯勒律治：

你的上一封来信充满了信任和友好的情感，使我不胜感激。希望你的心灵能在乡间生活中获得宁静！我最大的愿望就是你能稳定下来。请一定要继续给我写信。我和姐姐都读了你的来信，读你的信是很大的乐趣。尤其是当你以虔诚的语气写信时，读信给我们带来很大的乐趣——只是有时你的畅快直言和神秘主义的风格让我们感到被冒犯了，因为这更接近异端邪说的傲慢自大，而不是发自内心的虔诚所体现出来的谦卑。比如你上一封信中说到："上帝是在造人时就赋予了人类善与恶（我相信你仅是指好人与坏人），这其中体现着上帝的无所不在。尽管现在人类的智力相对而言会极大地提升，人类的影响力也会扩大，无论是好还是坏，但是柯勒律治啊，难道神灵和人类之间没有距离吗？你这一言论难

not, Coleridge, a distance between the Divine Mind and it, which makes such language **blasphemy**? Again, in your first fine **consolatory epistle** you say, 'You are a temporary sharer in human misery, that you may be an eternal **partaker** of the Divine Nature.' What more than this do those men say, who are for exalting the man Christ Jesus into the second person of an unknown **Trinity**, —men, whom you or I **scruple** not to call **idolaters**? Man, full of imperfections, at best, and subject to wants which momentarily remind him of dependence; man, a weak and ignorant being, **servile** from his birth 'to all the **skiey** influences,' with eyes sometimes open to discern the right path, but a head generally too dizzy to pursue it; man, in the pride of speculation, forgetting his nature, and hailing in himself the future God, must make the angels laugh. Be not angry with me, Coleridge; I wish not to **cavil**; I know I cannot instruct you; I only wish to remind you of that humility which best becometh the Christian character. God, in the New Testament (our best guide), is represented to us in the kind, condescending, amiable, familiar light of a parent: and in my poor mind 'try best for us so to consider of Him, as our heavenly father, and our best friend, without indulging too

道不是亵渎了神灵吗？还有，你在第一封给我们的文笔优美的问候信中说道："你只是暂时分享了人类的痛苦，却是神性永恒的共享者。"有些人把耶稣基督——一个凡人——追捧为未知的三位一体中的第二位。这些人你我都会毫不犹豫地视为偶像崇拜者，可是你的这番言论又和他们有什么区别呢？人类不管怎么说都是充满瑕疵的，容易被欲望左右，这些欲望无时无刻不在提醒他：自己是有依赖性的。人类是软弱又无知的一种生物，从出生之日起就带着奴性，就算达到人生顶峰时也是如此。人类有时睁开双眼辨明了正确的路，但却由于头昏脑涨而迷路。人类，因自身的思考能力而自豪，忘记了自己的根本，吹嘘自己是将来的上帝，天使听到了也会发笑的。柯勒律治，不要生我的气，我不是想要找你的茬。我知道我不能指挥你，只是想提醒你基督徒身上最优秀的一种品质——谦卑。上帝在《新约》（我们最好的指南）中展现的是仁慈、屈尊俯就、和蔼的我们熟悉的慈父形象。以我的拙见，我们最好把他看作我们的天父、我们最好的朋友，而不要沉溺于对上帝本质

bold conceptions of His Nature. Let us learn to think humbly of ourselves, and rejoice in the **appellation** of 'dear children,' **brethren,**' and 'co/heirs with Christ of the promises,' seeking to know no further.

I am not insensible, indeed I am not, of the value of that first letter of yours, and I shall find a reason to thank you for it again and again long after that **blemish** in it is forgotten. It will be a fine lesson or comfort to us, whenever we read it; and read it we often shall, Mary and I.

Accept our loves and best kind wishes for the welfare of yourself and wife, and little one. Nor let me forget to wish you joy on your birthday so lately past; I thought you had been older. My kind thanks and remembrances to Lloyd.

God love us all, and may He continue to be the father and the friend of the whole human race.

Sunday Evening.
C. Lamb

的大胆揣测之中。让我们学着把自己看得卑微一点吧，满足于"亲爱的孩子们"、"兄弟们"和"基督之诺言的共同继承人"这样的称号吧，不要试图知道更多了。

我不是不明白你的第一封信有多珍贵——我的的确确意识到了——当你信中的那一点点不足被遗忘很久以后，我会找机会一遍又一遍地感谢你的。无论什么时候读这封信，对你我都是最好的教训和安慰。我和玛丽也会经常读的。

请接受我们对您和夫人、孩子的爱和最美好的祝愿吧。我也不会忘记祝你生日快乐的，虽然你的生日刚刚过去。我以为你年纪会再大一点儿的。还有，请向劳埃德转达我的致谢和问好。

上帝爱着我们所有人，愿上帝永远是全人类的慈父和挚友！

查尔斯·兰姆于周日晚
1796年10月24日

单词解析 Word Analysis

debtor ['detə(r)] *n.* 债务人；借方

例 Bank officials argued that it is not their job to chase down every asset of every bank debtor.
银行官员称，他们没有义务追踪每个贷款户的每笔资产。

air [eə(r)] *n.* 神态；感觉；总体印象；氛围

例 Jennifer regarded him with an air of amusement.
珍妮弗觉得他很风趣。

consonant ['kɒnsənənt] *adj.* 一致的；符合的

例 I found their work very much consonant with this way of thinking.
我发现他们的工作与这种思维方式非常一致。

conceit [kən'siːt] *n.* 自负；自高自大

例 Pamela knew she herself was a good student, and that was not just a conceit.
帕梅拉知道自己是个好学生，而这绝不仅仅是自负。

pagan ['peɪgən] *n.* 异教徒，非基督教徒

例 The singing of Christmas carols is a custom derived from early dance routines of pagan origin.
唱圣诞颂歌的风俗源自异教徒早期的舞蹈仪式。

humility [hjuː'mɪləti] *n.* 谦逊；谦虚；谦恭

例 God will help you if you turn to Him in humility and trust.
如果你怀着一颗谦恭而信任的心向上帝求助，上帝会帮助你。

omnipresence [ˌɒmnɪ'prezns] *n.* 无所不在

例 God's omnipresence and the manifestation of his presence are two different things.
神的无所不在与他同在的表现是截然不同的事。

blasphemy ['blæsfəmi] *n.* 亵渎上帝（或宗教）的言行

例 He was found guilty of blasphemy and sentenced to three years in jail.
他被判犯有亵渎神明罪，刑期3年。

consolatory [kən'sɒlətəri] *adj.* 慰问的，可慰藉的

例 His words produced no consolatory effects.
他的话没有起到安慰作用。

epistle [ɪˈpɪsl] *n.* 书信；书信体

例 The genuineness of this epistle is not called in question.
书信的真实性没有受到质疑。

partaker [pɑːˈteɪkə] *n.* 参与者，分担者

例 And I do all things for the gospel's sake: that I may be made partaker thereof.
我所行的一切，都是为了福音，为了能与人共沾福音的恩许。

trinity [ˈtrɪnəti] *n.* （基督教圣父、圣子、圣灵的）三位一体

例 In the name of the holy and undivided Trinity, Father and Son and holy Spirit. Amen.
以神圣不可分割的三位一体，父亲和儿子和圣灵的名义，阿门。

scruple [ˈskruːpl] *vi.* 感到于心不安，有顾忌

例 She lied and did not even scruple about it.
她撒谎了并且没有迟疑过。

idolater [aɪˈdɒlətə] *n.* 偶像崇拜者

例 But does an idolater really believe that an idol is the actual god?
难道这个崇拜偶像的人真的相信这个偶像是神吗？

servile [ˈsɜːvaɪl] *adj.* 奴性的；逢迎的；恭顺的

例 They said she had a servile attitude to her employer.
他们说她对她的老板阿谀逢迎。

skiey [ˈskaɪɪ] *adj.* 天空的，天蓝色的，高耸云霄的

例 No one could reach such skiey achievements as him.
没有人能做到他这样巅峰的成就。

cavil [ˈkævl] *vi.* 挑剔，吹毛求疵

例 I don't think this is the time to cavil at the wording of the report.
我觉得现在还不是对报告的措辞较真的时候。

appellation [ˌæpəˈleɪʃn] *n.* 名称；称呼；称号

例 He earned the appellation "rebel priest."
他赢得了"反叛牧师"的称号。

brethren ['breðrən] *n.* （称呼教友或男修会等的成员）弟兄们

例 Sri Lankans share a common ancestry with their Indian brethren.
斯里兰卡人和他们的印度兄弟有共同的祖先。

blemish ['blemɪʃ] *n.* 污点；瑕疵

例 This is the one blemish on an otherwise resounding success.
如果没有这个小小的失误，这就是一次彻底的胜利。

语法知识点 *Grammar Points*

① **I only wish you were but settled.**

这个句子中"you were but settled"做"wish"的宾语从句，从句与现在事实相反，是虚拟语气，所以用动词的过去式。

例 He wishes he were good at martial arts so that he could protect his families.
他希望自己擅长武术，这样就可以保护家人了。

② **Man, full of imperfections, at best, and subject to wants which momentarily remind him of dependence.**

这个句子中"full of imperfections"做"man"的同位语，是一个形容词词组，同样的，名词词组也可以做同位语。

例 Li Lei, the tallest student in our class, is admired by all the girls in the class.
李雷，我们班最高的学生，受到了所有女生的喜爱。

③ **Man, a weak and ignorant being, servile from his birth 'to all the skiey influences,' with eyes sometimes open to discern the right path, but a head generally too dizzy to pursue it.**

这个句子中"too dizzy to pursue it"做"head"的后置定语。"too... to..."表示"太过……而不能……"。

例 This car is too old to drive.
这辆车太旧了，不能开了。

经典名句 *Famous Classics*

1. Where religion speaks, reason has only a right to hear. — Unknown
   宗教发言时，理智只有听的权利。——无名者

2. All the different religions are only so many religious dialects. — Lichtenberg
   各种不同的宗教不过是众多的信仰方言而已。——利齐登柏

3. One who recovers from sickness forgets about God. — Ethiopian Proverb
   病愈之后忘了上帝。——埃塞俄比亚谚语

4. I believe that our Heaven Father invented man because he was disappointed in monkey. — Mark Twain
   我相信，我们的天父之所以创造人是因为猴子使他失望了。——马克·吐温

5. If God did not exist, it would be necessary to invent Him. — Voltaire
   如果上帝并不存在，也有必要把他创造出来。——法国哲学家 伏尔泰

25 Michael Faraday to Sarah Barnard
迈克尔·法拉第致萨拉·巴纳德

Royal Institution, December 1820

My Dear Sarah,

It is astonishing how much the state of the body influences the powers of the mind. I have been thinking all the morning of the very delightful and interesting letter I would send you this evening, and now I am so tired, and yet have so much to do, that my thoughts are quite **giddy**, and run round your image without any power of themselves to stop and admire it. I want to say a thousand kind and, believe me, heartfelt things to you, but am not master of words fit for the purpose; and still, as I **ponder** and think on you, **chlorides**, trials, oil, Davy, steel, **miscellanea**, mercury, and fifty other professional fancies swim before and drive me further and further into the **quandary** of stupidness.

From your affectionate
Michael

我亲爱的萨拉：

身体状态对思维能力的影响是惊人的。我一整个早上都在想着晚上要寄给你一封愉快又有趣的信。现在的我十分疲劳，可还有那么多事情要做，以至于我的思绪乱糟糟的，它们绕着你的样子转来转去，却无力停下来欣赏它。我心中有千言万语想要对你说，相信我，它们都是发自肺腑的真心话，但我却找不到合适的话来表达。而且我一陷入对你深深的思念，氯化物、实验、油、戴维灯、钢、杂记、汞和50种其他有关我的职业的幻象就在眼前浮动，让我的思绪越飘越远，大脑陷入一片混乱。

你亲爱的
迈克尔
1820年12月于皇家研究院

Michael Faraday to Sarah Barnard
迈克尔·法拉第致萨拉·巴纳德

单词解析 Word Analysis

giddy ['gɪdi] *adj.* 头晕的；眩晕的
例 He felt giddy and light-headed.
他感到头晕目眩。

ponder ['pɒndə(r)] *vt.* 思索，衡量，沉思
例 I'm continually pondering how to improve the team.
我不断地在想如何提高队伍水平。

chloride ['klɔːraɪd] *n.* 氯化物
例 The fish or seafood is heavily salted with pure sodium chloride.
鱼或海鲜被抹了厚厚的纯盐腌制起来。

miscellanea [,mɪsə'leɪniə] *n.* 杂记，杂录
例 He has been reading the miscellanea written by this professor.
他最近在读这个教授写的杂记。

quandary ['kwɒndəri] *n.* 困境；窘境；左右为难的境地
例 The government appears to be in a quandary about how to do with so many people.
政府似乎陷入了左右为难的境地，不知道该拿这么多人怎么办。

语法知识点 Grammar Points

I have been thinking all the morning of the very delightful and interesting letter I would send you this evening, and now I am so tired, and yet have so much to do, that my thoughts are quite giddy, and run round your image without any power of themselves to stop and admire it.

这个句子是一个由"and"连接的并列句，第一个分句中"have been thinking"是现在完成进行时，表示从过去开始的一个动作一直持续到现在。

例 He has been working on a new program with his colleagues.
他最近在和同事一起进行一个新项目。

经典名句 Famous Classics

1. Good health is over wealth. — English proverb
   健康是最大的财富。——英国谚语

2. A light heart lives long. — William Shakespeare
   豁达者长寿。——威廉·莎士比亚

3. Care killed the cat. — William Shakespeare
   忧伤足以致命。——威廉·莎士比亚

4. Early to bed and early to rise, makes a man healthy, wealthy and wise. — Benjamin Franklin
   早睡早起，使人健康、富有、明智。——本杰明·富兰克林

5. Cheerfulness is the best promoter of health. — Thomas Addison
   快乐最利于健康。——爱迪生

6. Prevention is better than cure. — Charles Dickens
   预防胜过治疗。——查尔斯·狄更斯

7. Better wear out shoes than sheets. — English proverb
   宁愿把鞋子穿漏，不愿把床单磨破。——英国谚语

8. Life is like a river, movement against the moldy.
   生命像河流，运动防腐臭。

26 Percy Bysshe Shelley to John Keats
珀西·比希·雪莱致约翰·济慈

Pisa, 27 July 1820

My Dear Keats,

I hear with great pain the dangerous accident you have undergone, and Mr. Gisborne, who gives me the account of it, adds that you continue to wear a **consumptive** appearance. This **consumption** is particularly fond of people who write such good verses as you have done, and with the assistance of an English winter it can often indulge its selection. I do not think that young and amiable poets are bound to gratify its taste; they have entered into no bond with the Muses to that effect.

But seriously (for I am joking on what I am very anxious about) I think you would do well to pass the winter after so tremendous an accident, in Italy, and if you think it as necessary as I do, so long as you continue to find Pisa or its neighbourhood **agreeable** to you, Mrs. Shelley unites with myself in urging the request, that you would take up your residence with us. You might come by sea to Leghorn (France is not

我亲爱的济慈：

听说了你突然遭受病痛折磨，我心中十分难过。吉斯伯恩先生告知了我这一消息，说你还未病愈，还有结核病的症状。这种结核病尤其喜欢找像你一样诗写得好的人，再加上英国的冬天，使得它往往肆行无忌。我想，正处于青年时期又文质彬彬的诗人不应该满足它的口味，诗人们并没有和缪斯女神们订立过这样的契约。

但是说真的（我常以玩笑的口吻谈论自己很担心的事情），我认为在生了一场大病之后，你来意大利过冬是比较好的选择。如果你和我一样觉得有必要来意大利，只要你还喜欢比萨及其周边的地区，我和夫人都热切地邀请你来我家里住。你可以乘船去里窝那（法国没什么好看的，而且海上的空气尤其对虚弱的肺大有好处），那儿离我们家只有几英里远。无论怎样，你应该来

worth seeing, and the sea is particularly good for weak lungs), which is within a few miles of us. You ought, **at all events**, to see Italy, and your health, which I suggest as a motive, might be an excuse to you. I spare **declamation** about the statues, and the paintings, and the ruins, and what is a greater piece of **forbearance**, about the mountains streams and fields, the colours of the sky, and the sky itself.

I have lately read your 'Endymion' again and even with a new sense of the treasures of poetry it contains, though treasures poured forth with indistinct **profusion**. This, people in general will not endure, and that is the cause of the comparatively few copies which have been sold. I feel persuaded that you are capable of the greatest things, so you but will.

I always tell Ollier to send you copies of my books –'Prometheus Unbound'. I imagine you will receive nearly at the same time with this letter. 'The Cenci' I hope you have already received –It was **studiously** composed in a different style.

'Below the good how far! But far above the great.'

In poetry I have sought to avoid system and **mannerism**; I wish those who excel me in genius would pursue

意大利一趟。你的健康状况，在我看来，是来意大利的理由；对你来说，可能是推辞的借口。我忍着没有谈这里的雕塑、油画、遗迹，而忍住不谈这里的山川田野、天空及天空的颜色则花费了我更大的力气。

最近我重读了你的《恩底弥翁》，对诗中包含的诗意的宝藏有了新的认识，尽管它们层出不穷的涌现着。这一点，一般很少有人能接受，这也就是为什么这部作品销量相对较少的原因了。我相信你有能力创造出最伟大的作品，只要你愿意，就一定能行。

我一直嘱咐奥利尔寄给你《解放的普罗米修斯》的复印本。你可能会和这封信同时收到它。《钦契一家》——我希望你已经收到了——是我特意要体现一种不同的风格的。

"与'好'相距很远；但远在'伟大'之上。"

在写诗时，我极力避免模式化和风格化；我希望比我更有才华的人也能这样做。

不论你是留在英国还是来意大利，我都热切地希望你身体健康、开心快乐、事业成功。无论你在哪，无论你从事何种事业，我都是——

the same plan.

  Whether you remain in England, or journey to Italy, believe that you carry with you my anxious wishes for your health, happiness and success, wherever you are, or whatever you undertake, and that I am,

Yours sincerely,
P. B. Shelley

你真挚的
P. B. 雪莱
1820年7月27日于比萨

单词解析 Word Analysis

consumptive [kən'sʌmptɪv] *adj.* 患痨病的；患结核病的

例 He took her on tour of Europe, but the travel only hastened her consumptive decline and death.
他带她周游欧洲，但这趟旅行只是使她的结核病恶化更快，加速了她的死亡。

consumption [kən'sʌmpʃn] *n.* 肺病；肺痨；肺结核

例 Consumption used to be an obstinate disease.
肺结核过去是一种难治之症。

agreeable [ə'gri:əbl] *adj.* 令人愉快的，惬意的

例 I enjoyed an agreeable holiday this summer.
今年夏天我度过了一个愉快的假期。

at all events 不管怎样，无论如何

例 He is not clever, but at all events he works well.
他并不聪明，但不管怎样他做得很好。

declamation [ˌdekləˈmeɪʃn] *n.* 朗诵；雄辩

例 One traditional Chinese teaching method is declamation.
诵读教学是我国传统的语文教学方法。

forbearance [fɔː'beərəns] *n.* 忍耐，克制

例 All the Greenpeace people behaved with impressive forbearance and dignity.
所有绿色和平组织人士表现出了超乎寻常的克制和大度。

profusion [prə'fjuːʒn] *n.* 丰富，充沛

例 Olive groves, grapes, and citrus fruits grow in profusion.
橄榄、葡萄和柑橘类水果产量丰富。

studiously ['stjuːdɪəsli] *adv.* 刻意地；成心

例 When I looked at Clive, he studiously avoided my eyes.
当我朝克莱夫看去时，他刻意地避开了我的目光。

mannerism ['mænərɪzəm] *n.* （绘画、写作中）过分的独特风格

例 He used such mannerism as " er " and " uh " to fill in a pause.
他说话间歇时总爱用"呃""嗯"之类的话搭头。

语法知识点 Grammar Points

① **I do not think that young and amiable poets are bound to gratify its taste.**

这个句子中包含一个"that"引导的宾语从句。当宾语从句中表示否定时，否定词"not"等要提前到主句中。

例 I do not believe that such a morally good man could abuse animals.
我相信，道德正直的人是不会虐待动物的。

② **...and if you think it as necessary as I do, so long as you continue to find Pisa or its neighbourhood agreeable to you, Mrs. Shelley unites with myself in urging the request, that you would take up your residence with us.**

这个句子中"find"后跟了"Pisa or its neighbourhood"做宾语，以及"agreeable"做宾语补足语。"find + something/ somebody + adj./ n."是固定用法，表示"发现某人或某事……"。

例 We find living in Shanghai costly.
我们发现住在上海花费很高。

经典名句 Famous Classics

1. The finest poetry was first experience. — Emerson
   最优美的诗来自切身感受。——爱默生

2. Poetry the eldest sister of all arts, and parent of most. — William Congreve
   诗是一切艺术的长姊，大部分艺术的家长。——威廉·孔格雷夫

3. All good verses are like impromptus made at leisure. — Joubert
   一切优秀的诗篇都像闲时的即兴之作。——朱伯尔

4. A poem is the very image of life expressed in its eternal truth. — Shelley
   一首诗是永恒真理在人生幻象中的表露。——雪莱

5. Wisdom married to immortal verse. — Wordsworth
   智慧同不朽的诗篇匹配。——华兹华斯

6. Poets evermore are scant of gold. — E. Browning
   诗人始终缺少财富。——依·布朗宁

7. Painters and poets have always had an equal licence to dare anything. — Horace
   画家和诗人总是具有一种敢于面对一切的放纵性格。——贺拉斯

27 Abraham Lincoln to Miss Grace Bedell
亚伯拉罕·林肯致格蕾丝·比德尔小姐

October 19, 1860, Springfield, Illinois

My Dear Little Miss,

　　Your very agreeable letter of the 15th is received. I regret the necessity of saying I have no daughters. I have three sons —one seventeen, one nine, and one seven, years of age. They, with their mother, **constitute** my whole family. As to the **whiskers**, having never worn any, do not you think people would call it a piece of silly affection if I were to begin it now?

　　　　Your very sincere well-wisher
　　　　　　　　　　A. Lincoln

亲爱的小小姐：

　　我收到了你15日寄出的来信，看后感到非常高兴。我必须要说，很遗憾，我没有女儿。我有三个儿子——一个17岁，一个9岁，还有一个7岁。他们三个和他们的妈妈就是我全部的家人了。至于胡子，我还从来没有留过，如果我现在开始蓄胡子，你觉得人们会不会觉得我在犯傻？

　　　　　　　你真诚的祝愿者
　　　　　　　　　亚伯拉罕·林肯
　　　　　　　　1860年10月19日
　　　　于伊利诺斯州斯普林菲尔德

单词解析 Word Analysis

constitute [ˈkɒnstɪtjuːt] *vt.* 构成，组成
例 These acts constitute an interference in the internal affairs of other countries.
这种行动构成对别国内政的干涉。

whiskers [ˈwɪskə(r)s] *n.* 络腮胡子；连鬓胡子
例 The man has a savage-looking with large whiskers and a dirty face.
这个男人留着络腮胡，脸也没洗，看起来很粗野。

语法知识点 Grammar Points

> As to the whiskers, having never worn any, do you not think people would call it a piece of silly affection if I were to begin it now?

这个句子中"having never worn any"是动词的现在分词做状语，表示原因。

例 Realizing the importance of his image, the singer began to behave more carefully.
因为意识到了自己形象的重要性，这位歌手开始小心行事。

经典名句 Famous Classics

1. Childhood is measured out by sounds and smells and sights, before the dark hour of reason grows. — *The Boy in the Striped Pajamas*
   黑暗的理性萌发之前，孩童是通过声音、气味和画面来认知世界的。——《穿条纹睡衣的男孩》

2. Wisdom belongs to adults, pure belongs to children. — Pope
   智慧属于成人，纯真属于儿童。——蒲柏

3. Children like dirt, while their whole body and mind crave for sunshine like flowers. — Tagore
   儿童喜欢尘土，他们的整个身心像花朵一样渴求阳光。——泰戈尔

4. Where children are not, heaven is not. — Swinburne
   哪里无孩子，哪里便无天堂。——史文朋

5. A torn jacket is soon mended, but hard words bruise the heart of a child. — Longfellow
   衣服破了可以重补，粗鲁的话却会伤透孩子的心。——朗费罗

6. Of all nature's gift to the human race, what is sweeter to a man than his children. — Cicero
   大自然给予人类的礼物中，最美妙的莫过于人们的孩子了。——西塞罗

7. Childhood, whose very happiness is love. — Letitia Landon

141

童年时代的最大幸福是爱。——利蒂希娅·兰登

8. Childhood is a period of life reprocess in which human being survives for good. — Bernard Shaw
童年时代是生命在不断再生过程中的一个阶段，人类就是在这种不断的再生过程中永远生存下去的。——萧伯纳

读书笔记

28 Charles Darwin to W. D. Fox
查尔斯·达尔文致威廉·福克斯

Cambridge, March 1830

My Dear Fox,

I am through my Little-Go!!! I am too much exalted to **humble** myself by apologizing for not having written before. But I assure you before I went in, and when my nerves were in a shattered and weak condition, your injured person often rose before my eyes and **taunted** me with my idleness. But I am through, through, through. I could write the whole sheet full with this delightful word. I went in yesterday, and have just heard the joyful news. I shall not know for a week which class I am in. The whole examination is carried on in a different system. It has one grand advantage —being over in one day. They are rather strict, and ask a wonderful number of questions.

And now I want to know something about your plans; of course you intend coming up here: what fun we will have together; what beetles we will catch; it will do my heart good to go once more together to some of our old **haunts**.

亲爱的福克斯：

我通过预考啦！！！我现在欣喜若狂，以至于无法为之前没有给你写信而道歉。但我向你保证，考试前，每次我头脑崩溃、精神虚弱的时候，你委屈的样子就浮现在我眼前，使我不敢偷懒。但是我通过了，通过了，通过了！我能把整页纸都写满这欣喜的话语。我昨天参加的考试，今天才得知这一喜讯。一周之内我还不能知道自己是什么等级。这个考试采取了与其他考试完全不同的体系。它最大的好处就是——只用一天就考完了。主考官们非常严格，问了非常多的问题。

现在我想知道你是怎么打算的。你当然打算来我这里了，我们在一起会玩得很开心的，还可以捉甲壳虫，我也很喜欢再去逛一逛以前我们一起去过的地方。我有两个很优秀的跟我学习昆虫学的学生，我

I have two very promising pupils in Entomology, and we will make regular campaigns into the Fens. Heaven protect the beetles and Mr. Jenyns, for we won't leave him a pair in the whole country. My new cabinet is coming down, and a **gay** little affair it is.

And now for the time –I think I shall go for a few days to town to hear an opera and see Mr. Hope; not to mention my brother also, whom I should have no objection to see. If I go pretty soon, you can come afterwards, but if you settle your plans definitely, I will arrange mine, so send me a letter by return of post. And I charge you let it be favourable –that is to say, come directly. Holden has been **ordained**, and drove the coach out on the Monday. I do not think he is looking very well. Chapman wants you and myself to pay him a visit when you come up, and begs to be remembered to you. You must **excuse** this short letter, as I have no end more to send off by this day's post. I **long** to see you again, and till then,

My dear good old Fox,
Yours most sincerely,
C. DARWIN

Charles Darwin to W. D. Fox
查尔斯·达尔文致威廉·福克斯

单词解析 Word Analysis

humble ['hʌmbl] *vt.* 低声下气；谦逊；虚心

例 Ted's words humbled me.
泰德的话让我感到自惭。

taunt [tɔːnt] *vt.* 笑话；嘲笑；奚落

例 Other youths taunted him about his clothes.
其他年轻人笑话他的衣服。

haunt [hɔːnt] *n.* 常去的场所；消磨时光的去处

例 The pub is a favourite haunt of artists.
这家酒吧是艺术家最爱光顾的地方。

gay [geɪ] *adj.* 愉快的；快乐的

例 I am happy and free, in good health, gay and cheerful.
我快活自由，身体健康，积极乐观。

ordain [ɔːˈdeɪn] *vt.* 任命（某人）为牧师；授予（某人）圣职

例 He was ordained a Catholic priest in 1982.
他于1982年被任命为天主教司铎。

excuse [ɪkˈskjuːs] *vt.* 原谅；宽恕

例 Many people might have excused them for shirking some of their responsibilities.
很多人可能已经原谅了他们逃避责任的行为。

long [lɒŋ] *vi.* 渴望，极想

例 Steve longed for the good old days.
史蒂夫渴望重度昔日的美好时光。

语法知识点 Grammar Points

① I am too much exalted to humble myself by apologizing for not having written before.

这个句子中"too... to..."结构表示"太……以至于不能……"。

例 The letters are too small to see clearly.
这些字母太小了以至于看不清。

② **What fun we will have together.**

这个句子是一个"what"开头的强调句，句型为"what +名词+主语+谓语"。

例 What difficulties we have met with!
我们遇到的困难太大了！

经典名句 Famous Classics

1. Pain past is pleasure. — English proverb
   过去的痛苦就是快乐。——英国谚语

2. A bold attempt is half success. — Proverb
   勇敢的尝试是成功的一半。——谚语

3. Rejoicing in hope, patient in tribulation. — John Kennedy
   从希望中得到欢乐，在苦难中保持坚韧。——肯尼迪

4. Sweet are the uses of adversity. — William Shakespeare
   苦尽甘来。——莎士比亚

5. As a man sows, so he shall reap.
   种瓜得瓜，种豆得豆。

6. A young idler, an old beggar.
   少壮不努力，老大徒伤悲。

7. Old friends and old wines are best.
   陈酒味醇，老友情深。

8. Patience is the best remedy.
   忍耐是良药。

29 Alfred Tennyson to Queen Victoria
阿尔弗雷德·丁尼生致维多利亚女王

18 April 1886

I beg to offer to your Majesty the assurance of my own and my wife's **heartfelt** gratitude for your Majesty's most **gracious** letter of sympathy with us and ours and may I also add our sense of the kindness of Princess Beatrice in thinking of us.

We can have no further news we believe before Wednesday or Thursday but even in this most sad and solemn pause in our lives we feel deeply the state of public affairs.

Let it not be thought possible that England should **yield up** at the **bidding** of a band of robbers and **assassins** and those **deluded** by them all that is dearest to a nation.

We can never abandon the loyal Irish, never submit to give up any under your Majesty's rule whether loyal or disloyal to their ruin and our shame.

Differences of race should be a source of strength but not of weakness to a kingdom because of the diversities of gifts which it brings.

承蒙女王陛下在信中对我们夫妇二人以及子女的仁慈关怀，我们夫妇二人感恩不尽。还有比阿特丽丝公主对我们的挂念也让我们不胜感激。

周三和周四之前我们都没有进一步的消息。但即使在我们最悲伤和庄重的时间里，我们也深深关心着国家大事。

万万不能让外界以为英国会因为一群强盗和刺客以及被他们蛊惑的百姓的恐吓就放弃对它最宝贵的东西。

我们坚决不能放弃忠诚的爱尔兰人民，在陛下的统治下，决不能放弃任何一个臣民，不论他们忠诚于否。不然，就是对他们的毁灭和对我们的羞辱。

对一个国家来说，民族的不同应该是力量的源泉而不是软弱的根源，因为不同的民族会贡献出不同的智慧。

不管怎样地球上所有种族都信奉同一个道德准则，人类

At all events all **kindreds** of men on the face of the earth are under one moral law and all just human laws are founded on this. Where then is the **plea** for any special laws for Ireland? Customs there may be and let them be admitted.

If only this humiliating crisis cause conviction that the time for government by party has past, I think that your Majesty and your subjects will have a reason to be thankful that we have had past through it.

Men from natural tendencies will inevitably fall into something of party but let it be no longer a point of honour to **adhere** to a party. This point of honour is so easily **overstrained**.

Loyal and affectionate servant
Tennyson

所有公正的法律都建立在此之上。那么又有什么理由在爱尔兰实行特殊的法律呢？可能是由于特殊的风俗习惯，尊重他们的风俗就好了。

如果这一不光彩的危机导致人们相信政党统治的时代已经过去了的话，我认为陛下您和您的臣民们有理由庆贺我们成功渡过了这一危机。

人类由于天性使然，会不自觉地追随某个党派中去，但是不要让忠于党派成为一种光荣，人们往往会对此过度追求。

您忠诚可亲的仆人
丁尼生
1886年4月18日

单词解析 Word Analysis

heartfelt ['hɑːtfelt] *adj.* 衷心的；诚挚的

例 My heartfelt sympathy goes out to all the relatives.
我对所有的亲人表示由衷的慰问。

gracious ['greɪʃəs] *adj.* （尤指自己的上级和长者）仁慈的，宽厚的

例 She is a lovely and gracious woman.
她是位可爱又亲切的女人。

yield up 被迫放弃

例 Are the officials still refusing to yield up the town?
官员们仍然拒绝放弃那城池吗？

Alfred Tennyson to Queen Victoria
阿尔弗雷德·丁尼生致维多利亚女王

bidding ['bɪdɪŋ] *n.* 吩咐；命令

例 She is very clever at getting men to do her bidding!
她很善于让男人听她的吩咐！

assassin [ə'sæsɪn] *n.* 暗杀者，刺客

例 He saw the shooting and memorised the number of the assassin's car.
他目睹了枪击过程并记住了刺客的车牌号码。

delude [dɪ'luːd] *vt.* 欺骗，哄骗

例 We delude ourselves that we are in control.
我们骗自己说我们掌控着局面。

kindred ['kɪndrəd] *n.* （统称）家人，亲属

例 The offender made proper restitution to the victim's kindred.
违法者对受害人亲属给予了适当的补偿。

plea [pliː] *n.* 恳求，请求

例 Mr. Nicholas made his emotional plea for help in solving the killing.
尼古拉斯先生恳请帮助以解决这起凶杀案。

adhere [əd'hɪə(r)] *v.* 黏附；附着

例 We must adhere to the principle of making study serve the practical purpose.
我们必须坚持学以致用的原则。

overstrain ['əʊvə'streɪn] *v.* 使过度紧张，使工作过度

例 The doctor warned me not to overstrain my eyes.
医生警告我不要过度使用眼睛。

语法知识点 Grammar Points

Let it not be thought possible that England should yield up at the bidding of a band of robbers and assassins and those deluded by them all that is dearest to a nation.

这个句子中"that is dearest to a nation"是一个定语从句，修饰"all"。当先行词为"all、many、much、any"等词时，定语从句的关系代词只能用"that"。

例 There is not much time left that is needed for this project.
这个项目需要的时间所剩不多了。

经典名句 *Famous Classics*

1. The first method for estimating the intelligence of a ruler is to look at the men he has around him. — Niccolo Machiavelli
   估计一个统治者的智力，首先就是看看他身边的人。——尼科洛·马基雅弗利

2. Since a politician never believes what he says, he is surprised when others believe him. — Charles de Gaulle
   政客从来不相信自己说的话，所以，当别人相信他的话时，他必定会大吃一惊。——查尔斯·戴高乐

3. A man wrapped up in himself makes a very small bundle. — Benjamin Franklin
   一个只关心自己的人只能成就很小的事。——本杰明·富兰克林

4. The proper function of man is to live, but not to exist. — Jack London
   人应该生活，而非单纯生存。——杰克·伦敦

5. You shall have joy or you shall have power, said God; you shall not have both. — Emerson
   上帝说：你或者拥有欢乐，或者拥有权利，你不能两者兼而有之。——爱默生

6. You have freedom when you are easy in your harness. — Robert Frost
   在约束中能感到自如，那你就是自由的了。——罗伯特·弗罗斯特

7. Experience is the best teacher. — English proverb
   实践出真知。——英国谚语

30 Charles Dickens to Wilkie Collins
查尔斯·狄更斯致威尔基·柯林斯

London, 7 January 1860

My Dear Wilkie,

I have read this book with great care and attention. There cannot be a doubt that it is a very great advance on all your former writing, and most especially in respect of **tenderness**. In character it is excellent. Mr. Fairlie as good as the lawyer, and the lawyer as good as he. Mr. Vesey and Miss Halcombe, in their different ways, equally **meritorious**. Sir Percival, also, is most skillfully shown, though I doubt (you see what small points I come to) whether an man ever showed uneasiness by hand or foot without being forced by nature to show it in his face too. The story is very interesting, and the writing of it admirable.

I seem to have noticed, here and there, that the great pains you take express themselves a trifle too much, and you know that I always contest your **disposition** to give an audience credit for nothing, which necessarily involves the forcing of points on their attention,

亲爱的柯林斯：

我认认真真、仔仔细细地读了这本书。无须质疑，与你之前的写作相比，它是一个巨大的进步，尤其是它的笔法之细腻。这部书中塑造的角色也很精彩。费尔利先生和律师都塑造得栩栩如生。维西先生和海尔科姆小姐，虽然塑造手法不尽相同，但都值得称赞。珀西沃尔先生的塑造也很有技巧性，尽管我怀疑（你看我读的多仔细）是不是有人能在用手和脚表现自己不安的同时而忍住不在脸上表现出来。故事很有趣，写作手法也令人叫绝。

我似乎注意到了小说中处处流露出来的你的苦心雕琢，但这痕迹太重了些。你也知道，我一直不赞成你毫无保留地信任读者的倾向，这势必会导致把你的观点强加到读者身上。我也一直观察到了，当读者发现自己被灌输某种观点之后，会感到十分不忿，现在是这样，将来还

and which I have always observed them to resent when they find it out –as they always will and do. But on turning to the book again, I find it difficult to take out an instance of this. It rather belongs to your habit of thought and manner of going about the work. Perhaps I express my meaning best when I say that the three people who write the narrative in these proofs have a DISSECTIVE property in common, which is essentially not theirs but yours; and that my own effort would be to strike more of what is got that way out of them by collision with one another, and by the working of the story.

You know what an interest I have felt in your powers from the beginning of our friendship, and how very high I rate them? I know that this is an admirable book, and that it grips the difficulties of the weekly portion and throws them in a masterly style. No one else could do it half so well. I have stopped in every chapter to notice some instance of **ingenuity**, or some happy turn of writing; and I am absolutely certain that you never did half so well yourself.

So go on and prosper, and let me see some more, when you have enough (for your own satisfaction) to show me. I think of coming in to back you up if I can get an idea for my series of

是如此。但是一旦再次读这本书，又很难找到例子来证实这一点。这更取决于你的思维习惯和写作方式。可能我这样说会更清楚，书中的三个根据证据进行讲述的人物都具备剖析的能力，而这本质上不是他们的，而是你的。如果是我的话，我会努力通过他们彼此的冲突碰撞与错综复杂的故事情节来讲述推理的过程。

你知道，从我们结为朋友以来，我对你的创作能力就产生了十分浓厚的兴趣，对它的评价也很高。我知道这是一本值得钦佩的好书，也能游刃有余地应对每周连载的难题。换做其他人，连你的一半也达不到。我每一章都读到了一些别具一格的文字，或是令人兴奋的转折点。我也敢肯定，你之前的作品连这部小说的一半也达不到。

所以继续写吧，多多创作！当你有足够好的（你自己也满意的）作品时，再给我看更多的吧！等到我把《家常话》的有关事宜安排好后，我打算加入进来支持你的创作。上帝啊，拜托您，让我们能在不久后共同写作一个故事。我脑海中有一些可行的但未完全成形的想法，还处于一片模糊

gossiping papers. One of these days, please God, we may do a story together; I have very **odd** half-formed notions, in a mist, of something that might be done that way. –Ever affectionately.

之中，等待我们共同把它写成完整的作品。——永远关心你的朋友。

1860年1月7日于伦敦

单词解析 Word Analysis

tenderness ['tendənɪs] *n.* 亲切；柔和；细腻

例 Her friends' tenderness and sorrow must add to her distress.
她朋友们的体贴和伤心会增加她的苦恼。

meritorious [ˌmerɪ'tɔːriəs] *adj.* 值得称赞的

例 I had been promoted for what was called gallant and meritorious service.
我之所以得到提拔是由于立下了所谓的英勇卓越的功勋。

disposition [ˌdɪspə'zɪʃn] *n.* 倾向；意向

例 This has given him a disposition to consider our traditions critically.
这使他倾向以批判眼光看待我们的传统。

dissective [dɪ'sektɪv] *adj.* 仔细分析的，剖析的

例 We need to apply a dissective perspective to this issue.
对这一问题，我们要仔细剖析。

ingenuity [ˌɪndʒə'njuːəti] *n.* 独创力；聪明才智

例 He is a democrat with the skill, nerve, and ingenuity to push the limits of the possible.
他是一个手腕高超、富有胆识、足智多谋的民主党人，能够让不可能的事成为可能。

odd [ɒd] *adj.* 可得到的；可用的

例 Could I see you when you've got an odd moment?
你有空时，我能不能见见你？

语法知识点 *Grammar Points*

① I seem to have noticed, here and there, that the great pains you take express themselves a trifle too much.

这个句子中"you take"是省略了关系代词的定语从句，关系代词应为"that"，先行词为"pains"。由于关系代词"that"代替先行词"pains"在从句中作宾语，故"that"可省略。

例 This is the exact book I have read before.
   这就是我之前读过的那本书。

② You know what an interest I have felt in your powers from the beginning of our friendship, and how very high I rate them?

这个句子中有两个感叹句，一个以"what"引导，一个以"how"引导。"how"引导的强调句句型为"how + adj./ adv. + 主语 + 谓语"。

例 How quickly the Cheetah runs!
   猎豹跑得多快啊！

经典名句 *Famous Classics*

1. Something is learned every time a book is opened.
   开卷有益。

2. Life is not always a matter of holding good cards, but sometimes, playing a poor hand well. — Jack London
   人生不只是握有一副好牌，有时候也是把一副坏牌打好。——杰克·伦敦

3. It is our choices, that show us what we truly are, far more than our abilities. — J.K. Rowling
   是我们的选择，远大于我们的能力，真正展现出我们是什么样的人。——J. K.罗琳

4. I never could have done what I have done without the habits of punctuality, order, and diligence, without the determination to concentrate myself on one subject at a time. — Charles Dickens
   少了准时、规律及勤劳的习惯，少了一次只专心致志于一件事的决

心，我不可能得到今天的成就。——查尔斯·狄更斯

5. Courage is grace under pressure. — Ernest Hemingway
   勇气是压力下展现的优雅。——欧内斯特·海明威

6. It is the nature of man to rise to greatness if greatness is expected of him. — John Steinbeck
   人的天性是被期待卓越他就会成就卓越。——约翰·史坦贝克

7. Happiness is like a butterfly which, when pursued, is always beyond our grasp, but, if you will sit down quietly, may alight upon you. — Nathaniel Hawthorne
   快乐犹如一只蝴蝶，被追求时永远抓不到，但如果你安静地坐下，它可能会降落在你身上。——纳撒尼尔·霍桑

8. Little minds are tamed and subdued by misfortune, but great minds rise above them. — Washington Irving
   微小的人被厄运所驯服并压制，但伟大的人克服厄运。——华盛顿·欧文

读书笔记

31 Charlotte Brontë to Emily Brontë
夏洛特·勃朗特致艾米莉·勃朗特

> Stonegappe, 8 June 1839

Dearest Lavinia,

...I have striven hard to be pleased with my new situation. The country, the house, and the grounds are, as I have said, **divine**. But, alack-a-day! There is such a thing as seeing all beautiful around you –pleasant woods, winding white paths, green lawns, and blue sunshiny sky –and not having a free moment or a free thought left to enjoy them in. The children are constantly with me, and more **riotous**, **perverse**, unmanageable cubs never grew. As for correcting them, I soon quickly found that was entirely **out of the question**: they are to do as they like. A complaint to Mrs. Sidgwick brings only black looks upon oneself, and unjust, **partial** excuses to **screen** the children. I have tried that plan once. It succeeded so notably that I shall try it no more. I said in my last letter that Mrs. Sidgwick did not know me. I now begin to find that she does not intend to know me, that she cares nothing in the world about

最亲爱的莱维尼亚：

……我在很努力地让自己喜欢上这个新环境。像我说过的，这里的田野、房屋和庭院都是极美的。但是，天哪，竟然有这样的事情：你看着身边美丽的景色——长得好的树林、蜿蜒的白色小路、绿草坪和蓝色的明媚天空——却没有功夫也没有心思去欣赏它们。孩子们总是和我在一起，再没有比他们更吵闹任性、难以管教的淘气鬼了。至于要纠正他们的行为，我很快就发现那是不可能的：他们想做什么就一定要做。向西治威克太太抱怨只会给自己招来白眼，她只一味地用不公正又偏私的借口包庇孩子们。我曾经尝试过这一办法。但它实在是太有成效了，以至于我不会再这么做了。我在上一封信中说过，西治威克太太不了解我。我现在发现，她根本就不想了解我。她对我什么都不关心，只想挖

me except to contrive how the greatest possible quantity of labour may be squeezed out of me, and to that end she overwhelms me with oceans of needlework, yards of cambric to **hem**, muslin nightcaps to make, and, above all things, dolls to dress. I do not think she likes me at all, because I can't help being shy in such an entirely **novel** scene, surrounded as I have hitherto been by strange and constantly changing faces. I see now more clearly than I have ever done before that a private governess has no existence, who is not considered as a living and **rational** being except as connected with the **wearisome** duties she has to fulfill. While she is teaching the children, working for them, amusing them, it is all right. If she steals a moment for herself she is a **nuisance**... Mrs. Sidgwick expects me to do things that I cannot do –to love her children and be entirely devoted to them...

C. Brontë

空心思让我做最多的劳务活儿。为此，她几乎要把我淹没在针线活的海洋里，给亚麻布缝边、做细布睡帽，最过分的是要给一大堆布娃娃做衣服。我觉得她一点都不喜欢我，因为我在这全新的环境中不由自主地感到羞涩。至今为止，我周围都是陌生又不断变换的面孔。有一点我现在看得比以前更加清楚，那就是一个女家庭教师是没有存在感的，不被当作一个活生生的、有理性的人来看待，只被当作是完成乏味苦工的劳力。她在教导孩子们、为孩子们忙活、和孩子们玩耍时，一切都好。但她要是为自己偷得片刻的空闲，就是大逆不道……西治威克太太想要我做我办不到的事情——爱她的孩子们并且把自己全身心地奉献给他们……

夏·勃朗特
1839年6月8日于斯通盖普

单词解析 Word Analysis

divine [dɪ'vaɪn] *adj.* 绝妙的；非凡的；极美的

例 "Isn't it divine?" she said, "I wish I had the right sort of brooch to lend you for it."

"它是不是美极了？"她说道，"真希望我有合适的胸针可以借给你来搭配它。"

riotous ['raɪətəs] *adj.* 狂乱的；狂暴的

例 The organizers of the march were charged with assault and riotous assembly.
游行组织者被控侵犯人身及暴乱性非法集会。

perverse [pə'vɜːs] *adj.* 执拗的；任性的；不通情理的

例 She finds a perverse pleasure in upsetting her parents.
她让父母担惊受怕，从中取得任性的快乐。

out of the question 不可能的

例 For the homeless, private medical care is simply out of the question.
对于无家可归的人而言，私人医疗纯粹是天方夜谭。

partial ['pɑːʃl] *adj.* 偏爱的；偏袒的

例 Mollie confesses she is rather partial to pink.
莫莉承认她偏爱粉红色。

screen [skriːn] *vt.* 掩藏；庇护

例 Most of the road behind the hotel was screened by a block of flats.
宾馆后面的那条路大部分被一片公寓楼遮住了。

hem [hem] *vt.* 缝……的褶边

例 Each dress is hemmed and scrupulously checked for imperfections.
每条连衣裙都缝上了褶边，并经过严格的检查，不允许有任何瑕疵。

novel ['nɒvl] *adj.* 新奇的；异常的

例 Protesters found a novel way of demonstrating against steeply rising oil prices.
抗议者找到了抗议油价飞涨的新办法。

rational ['ræʃnəl] *adj.* 理性的；合理的

例 Mary was able to short-circuit her stress response by keeping her thoughts calm and rational.

玛丽能够保持头脑清醒理智，因而迅速做出反应。

Wearisome ['wɪərɪsəm] *adj.* 乏味的；令人疲劳的
- Sympathizing with him eventually becomes somewhat wearisome.
  对他的同情最终转变为些许的厌烦。

Nuisance ['njuːsns] *n.* 麻烦事；讨厌的人（或东西）
- He could be a bit of a nuisance when he was drunk.
  他醉酒时有点讨厌。

语法知识点 Grammar Points

① **The country, the house, and the grounds are, as I have said, divine.**

这个句子中"as"引导一个方式状语从句，意为"正如……"。
- The movie, as we have discussed, is worth watching.
  就像我们讨论的一样，这部电影值得一看。

② **I do not think she likes me at all, because I can't help being shy in such an entirely novel scene, surrounded as I have hitherto been by strange and constantly changing faces.**

这个句子中"can't help doing"意为"忍不住、不由自主地……"，是一个固定搭配。
- Seeing the homeless dog, he couldn't help sympathizing with it.
  看到这条流浪狗，他忍不住同情它。

经典名句 Famous Classics

1. You can get help from teachers, but you are going to have to learn a lot by yourself, sitting alone in a room. — Dr. Seuss, Children's Book Writer
   老师可以帮你的忙，但很多的学习你必须靠自己，独自坐在房里。——苏斯博士（童书作家）

2. Where parents do too much for their children, the children will not do much for themselves. — Elbert Hubbard, Writer

当父母为孩子做太多时，孩子就不会为自己做太多。——阿尔伯特·哈伯德（作家）

3. Children need models more than they need critics. — Joseph Joubert, Essayist
   孩子比较需要模范而非批评者。——儒贝尔（散文家）

4. What's done to children, they will do to society. — Karl Menninger, Psychiatrist
   对孩子做的事，他们也将对社会这么做。——卡尔·梅宁哲（精神科医师）

5. Education has for its object the formation of character. — Spencer
   教育的目的在于品德的培育。——斯宾塞

6. Education commences at the mother's knee, and every word spoken within the hearsay of children tends towards the formation of character. — Hosea Ballou
   教育始于母亲膝下，孩童耳听一言一语，均影响其性格的形成。——巴卢（英国教育家）

7. Genius without education is like silver in the mine. — Benjamin Franklin
   未受教育的天才，犹如矿中之银。——富兰克林

8. Example is always more efficacious than precept.
   身教胜于言教。

读书笔记

32 Mark Twain to W. D. Howells
马克·吐温致威廉·迪安·豪威尔斯

Elmira, Aug. 22, 1887

My Dear Howells,

How **stunning** are the changes which age makes in a man while he sleeps!

When I finished Carlyle's *French Revolution* in 1871, I was a Girondin; every time I have read it since, I have read it differently being influenced and changed, little by little, by life and environment (and Taine and St. Simon): and now I **lay** the book **down** once more, and recognize that I am a Sansculotte! –And not a pale, **characterless** Sansculotte, but a Marat. Carlyle teaches no such **gospel** so the change is in me –in my vision of the **evidences**.

People pretend that the *Bible* means the same to them at 50 that it did at all former **milestones** in their journey. I wonder how they can lie so. It comes of practice, no doubt. They would not say that of Dickens's or Scott's books. Nothing remains the same. When a man goes back to look at the house of his

亲爱的豪威尔斯：

人睡着的时候，年龄对他做出的改变多惊人啊！我在1871年读完卡莱尔的《法国革命史》的时候，是一个吉伦特派人；从那以后，每次我读这本书都会产生不同的感受，因为我在慢慢地被生活和环境影响改变（以及泰纳和圣西门的影响）。现在我再次读完这本书，发现自己竟然成了一个无套裤汉！——不是苍白无力、毫无个性的无套裤汉，而是马拉式的人物。卡莱尔没有传播这样的思想，所以这一改变的原因在我身上——来自于我对现象的观察。

人们假称《圣经》对自己的意义在50岁时和之前的各个人生关键期是一样的。我很好奇他们怎么能撒这样的谎。毫无疑问，这是习惯使然。他们不会这么评价狄更斯或司各特的书。没有什么是保持不变的。一个成年男人回头去看他

childhood, it has always **shrunk**: there is no instance of such a house being as big as the picture in memory and imagination call for. Shrunk how? Why, to its correct dimensions: the house hasn't been altered; this is the first time it has been in focus.

Well, that's loss. To have house and *Bible* shrink so, under the **disillusioning** corrected angle, is loss for a moment. But there are compensations. You **tilt** the tube skyward and bring planets and comets and corona flames a hundred and fifty thousand miles high into the field, which I see you have done, and found Tolstoi. I haven't got him in focus yet, but I've got Browning...

Yours Ever,

Mark

幼年住过的房子，总会觉得它变小了：没有房子是和他记忆或想象中的样子是一样大的。怎么会变小了呢？正确的看法是：房子从来没有变，只是人们这是第一次把它当作注意力的焦点。

好吧，那是一种损失。以纠正后的视角重新观察，人们会清醒地发现，房子和《圣经》都缩小是一种暂时的损失。但是并非没有补偿。你拿望远镜朝天上看，就能看到15万英里多高的行星、彗星和日冕。我看见你已经这么做了，而且看到了托尔斯泰。他还不在我的视野之中，但是我看到了布朗宁……

你永远的

马克

1887年8月22日于埃尔迈拉

单词解析 *Word Analysis*

stunning ['stʌnɪŋ] *adj.* 令人震惊的；令人惊奇万分的

例 The secret that the priest had confided to him was a stunning piece of news.

神父吐露给他的秘密真是条惊天大新闻。

lay down （通常指用完后）放下，搁下

例 Daniel finished the article and laid the newspaper down on his desk.

丹尼尔看完文章后把报纸放在他的书桌上。

Mark Twain to W. D. Howells
马克·吐温致威廉·迪安·豪威尔斯

characterless ['kærəktələs] *adj.* 缺乏特征的，平凡的
例 The town is boring and characterless.
这个小镇枯燥乏味，毫无特色。

gospel ['gɒspl] *n.* 福音音乐；真理，信条
例 It taught only materialism, the gospel of mammon.
它只是宣扬金钱至上的物欲主义。

evidence ['evɪdəns] *n.* 证据；迹象
例 There should be some tangible evidence that the economy is starting to recover.
应该有明显迹象表明经济开始复苏了。

milestone ['maɪlstəʊn] *n.* 里程碑；重大事件；重要阶段
例 He said the launch of the party represented a milestone in Zambian history.
他说该党的创立是赞比亚历史上的一个里程碑。

shrink [ʃrɪŋk] *v.* 缩水，收缩，缩小
例 The vast forests of West Africa have shrunk.
西非的大片森林面积已缩小了。

disillusion [ˌdɪsɪ'luːʒn] *v.* 使醒悟；使不再抱幻想
例 He said he had been bitterly disillusioned by his country's failure to change into a democracy.
他说他对他的国家未能实现民主变革极度失望。

tilt [tɪlt] *v.* （使）倾斜，倾侧
例 Mary tilted her head back so that she could look at him.
玛丽把头向后仰，以便能看到他。

语法知识点 *Grammar Points*

① People pretend that the *Bible* means the same to them at 50 that it did at all former milestones in their journey.v

这个句子中"that"引导一个定语从句,与"the same"连用表示"同一个"。

例 This is the same gift that I have sent you last time.
这和我上次送你的礼物一模一样。

② **This is the first time it has been in focus.**

这个句子是一个固定句型:"the first/second time... + 完成时",表示是某人第几次做某事。

例 It was the first time that I had been to Beijing.
那是我第一次去北京。

经典名句 Famous Classics

1. Good judgment comes from experience, and a lot of that comes from bad judgment. — Will Rogers, Humorist
明智的判断来自经验,而经验往往源自错误的判断。——威尔·罗杰斯(幽默演员)

2. Always do right. This will gratify some people and astonish the rest. — Mark Twain
永远做对的事,这将满足一些人,其他人则将感到惊奇。——马克·吐温

3. Humor is the secret of a surprise.
幽默的秘诀是出人意料。

4. Time take away everything; long will put your name in appearance, but personality change fate. — Plato
时间带走一切,长年累月会把你的名字、外貌、性格、命运都改变。——柏拉图

5. Be careful about reading health books. You may die of a misprint. — Mark Twain
阅读保健类书籍时要小心,你可能死于错误印刷。——马克·吐温

6. Always borrow money from a pessimist. He won't expect it back. — Oscar Wilde
跟悲观主义的人借钱吧,他不会指望你会还钱。——奥斯卡·王尔德

7. Silence is one of the hardest thing to refute. — John Billings, American humorist
沉默是最难驳斥的事物之一。——比林斯（美国幽默作家）

8. The greatest of faults is to be conscious of none. — Thomas Carlyle
最严重的错误莫过于不觉得自己有任何错误。——托马斯·卡莱尔

读书笔记

33 Eugene O' Neil to Beatrice Ashe
尤金·奥尼尔致比阿特丽丝·阿希

October 6, 1914

My Own,

Here I am back at the old dump once more feeling more lonely and **heartsick** than ever. It sure is hard to have to leave you in this way, and I am **fervently** praying to all the Gods that the time will soon come which will bring **surcease** of all these soul-aches which make life so horrible and full of pain. Ah, My Own, My Own, how I love you, and how the **relentless** hours drag their leaden feet when I am not with you!

I am thinking of last night and of all the wonder which is you, and my great desire moans from the depths of its **abysmal** aloneness: "Give us, ah give us but yesterday!"

Life has become for me a **phantom** show in which there are but two realities –you and my love for you. All else is misty shadow of illusion, vain **fretting** most valueless. I exist as I am reflected in you. I can only endure myself when I see my image in your eyes –in your gray pool does this Narcissus see himself,

我的宝贝：

我又回到了脏乱的老地方，感到了比以往更强烈的孤独和沮丧。以这样的方式离开你是很困难的，我不停地向诸神祈祷，让这相思的煎熬快些结束吧，让生活不再这么痛苦。啊，我的宝贝，我的宝贝，我多么爱你，我们不在一起的时候，时间过得多慢多难熬啊！

我在回想昨晚和所有的美妙，也就是你，我最大的愿望在从我内心深处的孤独中发出呻吟："把昨天给我们吧，给我们吧！"

我的生活变成了一场缥缈的幻影，其中只有两样东西是真实的——你和我对你的爱。其他的都是迷雾般的幻觉、毫无意义和价值的烦恼。只有你眼中的我才是真实存在的。只有我看着你、你也看着我时，我才能忍受自己——在你灰色的眸子里，我这位纳西索斯看见了自己、欣赏自己，对能出

Eugene O' Neil to Beatrice Ashe
尤金·奥尼尔致比阿特丽丝·阿希

and admire, and feel so proud to be there.

"It's a long, long way to Tipperary" and countless **aeons** before my birthday when I shall again feel your soft warm lips on mine. I could shake the skies with my fruitless cries, **gnash** my sharp (according to you) teeth with my rage at fate –but what's the use? Time will pass however slowly, and again I shall hold you in my arms, Dear One, Most Adorable of All Women. A long kiss! Good night.

Gene

现在那儿感到骄傲。

"去蒂帕雷里的路很漫长、很漫长。"离我的生日还有很久很久,还要隔上很久才能再次感受到你温柔的吻。我没有结果的哭喊能够撼动天地,因为命运而气得咬牙切齿(这取决于你)——但是这有什么用呢?无论多慢,时间总会过去的,我就能再次拥你入怀中了,亲爱的,你是我的唯一,天底下最可爱的女子。长吻!晚安。

金
1914年10月6日

单词解析 Word Analysis

heartsick ['hɑːtsɪk] *adj.* 闷闷不乐的,愁眉苦脸的
例 Losing his lover makes him heartsick and depressed.
失去了爱人让他心灰意冷、意志消沉。

fervently ['fɜːvəntlɪ] *adv.* 热烈地,热情地
例 I fervently hope he recognizes and understands the burden that's on his shoulders.
我热诚地希望他能认识到并懂得自己肩负的重任。

surcease [sɜːˈsiːs] *n.* 停止
例 I hope tomorrow's negotiation will bring surcease to the conflict.
我希望明天的谈判能够解决冲突。

relentless [rɪˈlentləs] *adj.* 不懈的;坚韧的
例 He was the most relentless enemy I have ever known.
他是我所遇到的最不屈不挠的敌手。

abysmal [əˈbɪzməl] *adj.* 深不可测的

例 The scene in which two men fought on an abysmal cliff gave me a deep impression.
两个男人在万丈悬崖上打斗的场面给我留下了深刻印象。

phantom [ˈfæntəm] *n.* 幻影；幽灵

例 The phantom used to appear unexpectedly, but mostly during the winter.
那个幽灵过去常常出人意料地出现，但是大多在冬季。

fret [fret] *v.* 苦恼；烦躁；焦虑不安

例 Why should you fret over the things that won't happen?
何必为不可能发生的事情烦恼?

aeon [ˈiːən] *n.* 极漫长的时期；千万年

例 Aeons ago, there were deserts where there is now fertile land.
现在是肥沃土地的地方在很久很久以前曾是一片片沙漠。

gnash [næʃ] *vt.* （因愤怒或痛苦等）咬（牙）

例 If you couldn't attend either of the concerts and are currently gnashing your teeth at having missed out, don't despair.
如果这两场音乐会你都未能参加并且正在为错失机会而懊恼的话，别灰心。

语法知识点 Grammar Points

① **Here I am back at the old dump once more feeling more lonely and heartsick than ever.**

这个句子中"feeling"是"feel"的现在分词形式，在句中做伴随状语。动词的现在分词可以做伴随状语，表示与主句动作同时发生。

例 He sits there on the bench alone thinking about his teacher's words.
他独自坐在长椅上，想着老师说过的话。

② **I exist as I am reflected in you.**

这个句子中"as"引导一个时间状语从句，表示"当……时候"。

例 As his mother came home, he ran immediately to the door to welcome her.
妈妈回家的时候，他立马跑到门口迎接她。

经典名句 *Famous Classics*

1. Your task is not to seek for love, but merely to seek and find all the barriers within yourself that you have built against it. — Jalal ad-Din Muhammad Rumi, Poet
   你的任务不是寻找爱，而是寻找并发现所有你内在所建筑不让爱进来的障碍。——贾拉尔·阿德-丁·穆罕默德·鲁米（诗人）

2. To love means loving the unlovable. To forgive means pardoning the unpardonable. Faith means believing the unbelievable. Hope means hoping when everything seems hopeless. — Gilbert K. Chesterton, Writer
   爱意味着爱不该被爱的，原谅意味着宽恕不可宽恕的，信念是相信不可信的，希望意味着万念俱灰时仍抱着希望。——吉尔伯特·切斯特顿（作家）

3. Being in love is not a choice we make once; it's a choice we make multiple times. — Bruce Feiler, Writer
   相爱不是一个一次性的选择，而是很多次的选择。——布鲁斯·法勒（作家）

4. Keep love in your heart. A life without it is like a sunless garden when the flowers are dead. — Oscar Wilde, Writer
   把爱放在心里，没有爱的人生如同花园没有阳光时花朵都死去。——奥斯卡·王尔德（作家）

5. Where there is love there is life. — Mahatma Gandhi, Statesman
   有爱的地方就有生命。——圣雄·甘地（政治家）

6. Love begets love, love knows no rules, this is same for all. — Virgil, Poet
   爱产生爱，爱没有规则，这适用于所有人。——维吉尔（诗人）

7. Nuptial love makes mankind; friendly love perfects it; but wanton love corrupts and debases it. — Francis Bacon, Philosopher
   婚姻之爱创造人类，友谊之爱使其完美，但不负责的爱腐蚀并使人类堕落。——法兰西斯·培根（哲学家）

8. Love is that condition in which the happiness of another person is essential to your own. — Robert Heinlein, Science Fiction Writer
   爱是当另一个人的快乐决定性地影响你自己的快乐。——罗伯特·海莱因（科幻小说家）

读书笔记

34 William James to His Students
威廉·詹姆斯致他的学生

Cambridge, April 6, 1896

Dear Young Ladies,

I am deeply touched by your **remembrance**. It is the first time anyone ever treated me so kindly, so you may well believe that the impression on the heart of the lonely sufferer will be even more **durable** than the impression on your minds of all the teachings of *Philosophy 2A*. I now perceive one immense **omission** in my *Psychology*, —the deepest principle of Human Nature is the **craving** to be appreciated, and I left it out altogether from the book, because I had never had it gratified till now. I fear you have let loose a **demon** in me, and that all my actions will now be for the sake of such rewards. However, I will try to be faithful to this one unique and beautiful **azalea** tree, the pride of my life and delight of my existence. Winter and summer will I tend and water it –even with my tears. Mrs. James shall never go near it or touch it. If it dies, I will die too; and if I die, it shall be planted on my grave.

亲爱的年轻女士们：

你们送的纪念品让我深受感动。这是头一回有人对我这么好，所以你们大可放心，你们在我这个饱受孤独折磨的人心上留下的印象，比《哲学2A》在你们头脑中留下的印象还要深。我现在意识到，我教授的《心理学》忽视了一项重要的内容——人性最根本的本质在于被人欣赏的需求。我在书本上完全没有提这一点，因为我的这一需求在此之前从来没有被满足过。恐怕你们现在把我心中的这个恶魔释放出来了，我从今往后所做的所有事情都要以获得别人的赞赏为目的。然而，我会尽力忠于这一株独一无二的漂亮的杜鹃花。它是我生命的骄傲和生存的乐趣。无论冬天还是夏天，我都会悉心照料它，给他浇水——甚至用我的眼泪灌溉它。我不会让詹姆斯太太靠近它或触碰它。如果这棵树死了，我也会

Don't take all this too **jocosely**, but believe in the extreme pleasure you have caused me, and in the affectionate feelings with which I am and shall always be faithfully your friend,

Wm. James

死的；如果我死了，它会被种在我的坟墓上。

　　不要把这完全当作玩笑话，要相信你们给我带来的巨大的喜悦。怀着深厚的情感，我是并且永远是你们忠诚的朋友——

威廉·詹姆斯
1896年4月6日于坎布里奇

单词解析 Word Analysis

remembrance [rɪ'membrəns] *n.* 纪念品；纪念物

例 The cenotaph stands as a remembrance of those killed during the war.
矗立着的纪念碑是对战争中死难者的纪念。

durable ['djʊərəbl] *adj.* 持久的；耐用的

例 She bought herself a pair of durable trousers.
她给自己买了一条耐穿的裤子。

omission [ə'mɪʃn] *n.* 遗漏；疏忽

例 There were a number of errors and omissions in the article.
这篇文章中有多处错误和疏漏。

craving ['kreɪvɪŋ] *n.* 渴望，渴求

例 His craving for wealth led him on to crime.
他对财富的渴望带领他走上了犯罪的道路。

demon ['diːmən] *n.* 恶魔；魔鬼

例 His private demons drove him to drink excessively for many years.
他个人的心魔让他多年以来酗酒度日。

azalea [ə'zeɪliə] *n.* 杜鹃花

例 The mountains are ablaze with azalea, wistaria.
整个山上都长满了杜鹃花和紫藤花。

jocosely [dʒəʊkəʊslɪ] *adv.* 说玩笑地，诙谐地
- He takes all the hurting words jocosely.
  他对所有伤人的话语一笑视之。

语法知识点 Grammar Points

① It is the first time anyone ever treated me so kindly...

这个句子中"the first time"与完成时搭配是一个固定用法。"anyone ever treated me so kindly"是修饰"time"的同位语从句，从句连词为"that"，在习惯用语中常常可以省略。

- He is so excited because this is the first time that he has been to America.
  他很兴奋，因为这是他第一次去美国。

② ...and I left it out altogether from the book, because I had never had it gratifies till now.

这个句子中"because"引导一个原因状语从句，从句中"never、no、not"等否定词与till或until搭配表示"直到……才"。

- I didn't recognize him until he took off his sunglasses.
  他摘掉墨镜，我才认出他来。

经典名句 Famous Classics

1. The more you recognize and express gratitude for the things you have, the more things you will have to express gratitude for. — Zig Ziglar, Motivational Speaker
   你愈认可并对拥有的东西表达感恩，你愈会有更多东西表达你的感恩。——吉格·金克拉（励志演说家）

2. Feeling gratitude and not expressing it is like wrapping a present and not giving it. — William Arthur Ward, Scholar
   心存感谢但不表达它，如同裹起礼物但不送出去。——威廉·亚瑟·沃德（学者）

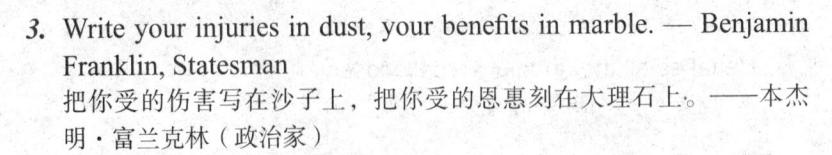

3. Write your injuries in dust, your benefits in marble. — Benjamin Franklin, Statesman
   把你受的伤害写在沙子上，把你受的恩惠刻在大理石上。——本杰明·富兰克林（政治家）

4. Gratitude is the sign of noble souls.
   感恩是精神高尚的标志。

5. Happiness is not something you postpone for the future; it is something you design for the present. — Jim Rohn, Author
   快乐不是你延后将来要做的事，而是你计划现在要做的事。——吉姆·罗恩（励志作家）

6. In every triumph there's a lot of try. — Frank Tyger, Cartoonist
   每个胜利背后都有许多尝试。——法兰克·泰格尔（插画家）

7. Don't worry when you are not recognized, but strive to be worthy of recognition. — Abraham Lincoln
   不要担心你没被认出，努力成为值得赏识的人。——亚伯拉罕·林肯

8. Be a life long or short, its completeness depends on what it was lived for. — David Starr Jordan, Scientist
   生命不论长短，它的完整度取决于生活的目的。——大卫·乔登（科学家）

读书笔记

35 Charlotte Brontë to Ellen Nussey
夏洛特·勃朗特致爱伦·纳西

Roe-Head, Oct. 1836

Weary with a day's hard work – during which an unusual degree of stupidity has been displayed by my promising pupils I am sitting down to write a few hurried lines to my dear Ellen. Excuse me if I say nothing but nonsense, for my mind is exhausted, and **dispirited**. It is a stormy evening and the wind is uttering a continual moaning sound that makes me feel very **melancholy** –At such times, in such moods as these Ellen it is my nature to seek repose in some calm, tranquil idea and I have now **summoned up** your image to give me rest. There you sit, upright and still in your black dress and white scarf –your pale, marble-like face –looking so serene and kind –just like reality –I wish you would speak to me. If we should be separated, if it should be our **lot** to live at a great distance and never to see each other again, in old age how I should call up the memory of my youthful days and what a melancholy pleasure I should feel in dwelling on

经过一天的辛劳，我疲惫不堪（我那些"有希望的"学生们表现出的愚蠢真是不同凡响），现在正坐下来给我亲爱的爱伦草草地写几行信。请原谅我，如果我说了什么胡话的话，因为我已经精疲力竭、情绪低沉。这是一个暴风雨的夜晚，风在发出持续的低吟，让我感觉很悲伤——爱伦，在这样的时刻和这样的心情里，我要想一些平静安宁的事物是人之常情。现在，你的样子浮现在我的脑海里，给我以宁静。你端坐在那里，穿着黑色衣衫，系着白色围巾——你那苍白如大理石的脸——看起来是如此的安详和善——就像真人一样——你要是能开口说话就好了。如果我们会被分开，如果我们注定要隔着很远的距离、再也见不到彼此的话，到老年时，我该怎样回忆我的青葱岁月呢？而当我思念着早年的好友爱伦·纳西时，心中又

the recollection of my early friend Ellen Nussey!

If I like people it is my nature to tell them so and I am not afraid of offering incense to your vanity. It is from religion that you derive your chief charm and may its influence always preserve you as pure, as **unassuming** and as benevolent in thought and deed as you are now. What am I compared to you! I feel my own utter worthlessness when I make the comparison. I'm a very coarse commonplace wretch!

Ellen, I have some qualities that make me very miserable, some feelings that you can have no participation in – that very few people in the world can at all understand. I don't pride myself on these peculiarities. I strive to conceal and suppress them as much as I can, but they burst out sometimes and then those who see the explosion despise me and I hate myself for days afterwards. We are going to have prayers so I can write no more of this trash yet it is too true.

I must send this note **for want of** a better. I don't know what to say. I've just received your epistle and what accompanied it. I can't tell what should induce your sisters to waste their kindness on such a one as me. I'm obliged to them and I hope you'll tell them so –I'm **obliged to** you also,

是怎样的忧伤和快乐啊!

如果我喜欢谁,就会直接告诉他,这是我的本性,我也不怕这会引起你的虚荣心。你的魅力主要来自宗教,希望宗教对你的影响能一直持续下去,希望你的思想与行为能像现在一样永远纯净、真诚、和善。和你比起来,我又算什么呢?每当我做这样的比较的时候,就感觉到了自己的毫无价值。我只是一个极其粗野平庸的凡人罢了。

爱伦,我身上的某些特质使我非常痛苦,有些感觉是你没有体会过的——世上很少有人能够理解。我不以这些不同之处而自豪,我极力想隐藏和压抑它们,但它们还是有时会爆发出来,然后见过它们爆发的人都会鄙视我,之后我也会连着几天陷入自厌的情绪当中。我们要去做祷告了,所以我可以不写这些废话了,然而它们都是千真万确的。

想不出更好的,我只能寄给你这封便笺了。我不知道该说什么。我刚刚才收到了你的书信和随信寄来的礼物。我不知道是什么让你的姐妹们把善意浪费在我这样的一个人身上。我很感激她们,希望你能如实转告——我也很感激你,更多是因为你的信而不是礼

more for your note than for your present –the first gave me pleasure, the last something very like pain. Give my love to both your sisters and my thanks. The bonnet is too handsome for me. I dare write no more. When shall we meet again?

C. Brontë

物——信给我带来快乐，礼物则更像痛苦。请转达给你的姐妹们我的爱与感谢吧！那顶贝雷帽太好看了，不适合我。我不敢再写下去了。我们什么时候能再次见面呢？

夏·勃朗特
1836年10月于罗海德

单词解析 Word Analysis

weary ['wɪəri] *adj.* 疲倦的；困乏的

例 He managed a weary smile.
他勉强挤出了一丝疲倦的笑容。

dispirited [dɪ'spɪrɪtɪd] *adj.* 沮丧的；没有精神的

例 I left eventually at six o'clock feeling utterly dispirited and depressed.
我一直到6点才极度沮丧和郁闷地离去。

melancholy ['melənkəli] *adj.* 忧郁的；悲伤的

例 The songs start soft and melancholy.
歌声轻柔而忧伤地响起。

summon up 唤起；使想起

例 The oddest events will summon up memories.
那些非常稀奇古怪的事情会唤起人们的记忆。

lot [lɒt] *n.* 命运；生活状况

例 She tried to accept her marriage as her lot in life but could not.
她想认命接受这段婚姻，但却做不到。

unassuming [ˌʌnə'sjuːmɪŋ] *adj.* 谦逊的，不装腔作势的

例 He was a small and to all appearances an unassuming man.
他个子小，看上去不张扬。

for want of 因缺乏……

例 Many of them had gone into teaching for want of anything better to do.
因为没有更好的工作,他们当中很多人做了教师。

be obliged to somebody 感激;感谢

例 We should be obliged to you for your assistance in this matter.
蒙您大力协助,我们将深表感激。

语法知识点 Grammar Points

① **Weary with a day's hard work –during which an unusual degree of Stupidity has been displayed by my promising pupils I am sitting down to write a few hurried lines to my dear Ellen.**

这个句子中"weary with a day's hard work"是一个形容词词组,中心词为"weary",做"I"的同位语,补充说明主语的状态。

例 He, defeated by his opponent, stands up again.
他被对手打倒后又站起来了。

② **It is from religion that you derive your chief charm...**

这个句子是一个强调句,强调"from religion",句型为"it is... that..."。

例 It is in a better environment that you have lived.
你的居住环境是真的更好了。

③ **...may its influence always preserve you as pure, as unassuming and as benevolent in thought and deed as you are now.**

这是一个以"may"开头的祈使句,意为"希望",其后跟动词原形。

例 May our friendship live long!
愿我们的友谊长存!

经典名句 Famous Classics

1. Jealousy contains more of self-love than of love. — Francois de La Rochefoucauld, Writer

嫉妒藏着对自己的爱，多于对他人的爱。——法兰索瓦·德·拉罗希福可（作家）

2. It is better to be hated for what you are than to be loved for what you are not. — André Gide, Writer
   宁可做自己而被讨厌，不要假装而被喜爱。——安德烈·纪德（作家）

3. The secret of a happy marriage is finding the right person. You know they're right if you love to be with them all the time. — Julia Child, Chef
   快乐婚姻的秘密是找到对的人，如果你喜欢一直和他在一起，他就是对的人。——朱丽亚·查尔德（厨师）

4. A successful marriage requires falling in love many times, always with the same person. — Mignon McLaughlin, Writer
   成功的婚姻需要和同一个人多次堕入爱河。——米格恩·麦克劳琳（作家）

5. One's life has value so long as one attributes value to the life of others, by means of love, friendship, indignation and compassion. — Simone de Beauvoir, Writer
   只要一个人通过爱、友谊、义愤或怜悯，为他人的生活创造价值，他的生活就有价值。——西蒙·波娃（作家）

6. Never let fear or shame keep you from celebrating the unique people that you are. — Kristen Anderson-Lopez
   绝不要让害怕或羞怯阻止你欣赏自己的独一无二。——克莉丝汀·安德森–罗培兹

7. We can do no great things, only small things with great love. — Mother Teresa
   我们不能做伟大的事，只能以伟大的爱来做小事。——德蕾莎修女

8. Darkness cannot drive out darkness: only light can do that. Hate cannot drive out hate: only love can do that. — Martin Luther King
   黑暗无法驱走黑暗，只有光线可以；仇恨无法驱走仇恨，只有关爱可以。——马丁·路德·金

36 Edgar Allan Poe to Sarah Helen Whitman
埃德加·爱伦·坡致萨拉·海伦·惠特曼

Steamboat, New York, November 14, 1848

My Own Dearest Helen,

So kind, so true, so generous –so **unmoved** by all that would have moved one who had been less than angel – **beloved** of my heart of my imagination of my intellect –life of my life –soul of my soul –dear, dearest Helen, how shall I ever thank you as I ought.

I am calm and **tranquil** but for a strange shadow of coming evil which haunts me I should be happy. That I am not **supremely** happy, even when I feel your dear love at my heart, terrifies me. What can this mean?

Perhaps however it is only the necessary reaction after such terrible excitements.

It is 5 o'clock and the boat is just being made fast to the **wharf**. I shall start in the train that leaves New York at 7 for Fordham. I write this to show you that I have not dared to break my promise to you.

And now dear dearest Helen, be true to me...

我最亲爱的海伦：

你是如此善良、如此真诚、如此慷慨——你是如此的坚贞，不为任何凡人向往的东西所动——我的心灵、想象和智慧的挚爱——我生命的生命——我灵魂的灵魂——亲爱的，最亲爱的海伦，我该怎样感谢你啊！

我很平静、镇定，但是有一道厄运即将来临的阴影萦绕在心间，要是能不为它所扰，我就很开心了。即使我能感受到你对我的爱，但我还没有感到至高的快乐，这使我恐慌。这意味着什么呢？

也许这只是兴奋过度带来的必然反应吧。

现在是5点钟了，船在加速向码头驶去。我要登上从纽约去福德海姆的火车了。我不敢违背我们的诺言，故写下此信。

现在，亲爱的、最亲爱的海伦，请真诚地对待我吧……

1848年11月14日于纽约汽轮上

Edgar Allan Poe to Sarah Helen Whitman
埃德加·爱伦·坡致萨拉·海伦·惠特曼

单词解析 Word Analysis

unmoved [ˌʌnˈmuːvd] *adj.* 坚定的，不动摇的

例 Despite the enemy's heavy gunfire, our troops stood steadfast and unmoved.
尽管敌人炮火猛烈，我们的部队岿然不动。

beloved [bɪˈlʌvd] *adj.* 亲爱的；被热爱的

例 The rose is the most romantic of flowers, beloved of poets, singers, and artists.
玫瑰是最浪漫的花，深受诗人、歌手和艺术家的喜爱。

tranquil [ˈtræŋkwɪl] *adj.* 宁静的；平静的

例 The place was tranquil and appealing.
那个地方恬静宜人。

supremely [suːˈpriːmli] *adv.* 极其，极为

例 She gets on with her job and does it supremely well.
她继续她的工作，并且做得非常出色。

wharf [wɔːf] *n.* 码头，停泊处

例 The ship lies alongside the wharf.
那艘船停靠在码头边。

语法知识点 Grammar Points

① **but for a strange shadow of coming evil which haunts me I should be happy.**

这个句子中"but for"是一个介词短语，意为"要不是"，通常暗含虚拟语气。

例 But for his advice, the boy wouldn't learn to ride a bike in such a short time.
要不是他的建议，这个男孩不会在这么短的时间内学会骑自行车。

② **That I am not supremely happy, even when I feel your dear love at my heart, terrifies me.**

这个句子中"that"引导一个主语从句,在句中不做成分,但也不可省略。

例 That she is coming soon surprises me.
我很惊讶她很快就来。

经典名句 Famous Classics

1. Love is patient; love is kind; love is not envious or boastful or arrogant or rude. — *Bible*
   爱是耐心,爱是和蔼,爱不是嫉妒或自夸或憍慢或粗野。——《圣经》

2. However difficult life may seem, there is always something you can do and succeed at. — Stephen Hawking
   不管生活多么困难,总是有你可以做以及取得成功的事。——史蒂芬·霍金

3. Life is like riding a bicycle. To keep your balance, you must keep moving. — Albert Einstein
   人生就像骑脚踏车,为了保持平衡,你必须不断往前走。——爱因斯坦

4. Many of life's failures are experienced by people who did not realize how close they were to success when they gave up. — Thomas Edison
   很多人失败,因为他们不知道他们放弃时距离成功是多么的近。——爱迪生

5. My life didn't please me, so I created my life. — Coco Chanel
   我的生活不能取悦我,所以我创造了自己的生活。——可可·香奈儿

6. Nothing in life is to be feared, it is only to be understood. Now is the time to understand more, so that we may fear less. — Marie Curie
   生命里没有要畏惧的,只有要了解的,我们应该了解多一些,才能畏惧少一点。——居里夫人

7. Perseverance is not a long race; it is many short races one after another. — Walter Elliott, Clergyman
   坚持不是一个长跑,它是很多一个接一个的短跑。——沃尔特·埃利奥特(传教士)

37 William Cullen Bryant to Sarah S. Bryant
威廉·卡伦·布莱恩特致萨拉·布莱恩特

June, 1821

Dear Mother,

I hasten to send you the **melancholy** intelligence of what has lately happened to me.

Early on the evening of the eleventh day of the present month I was at a neighboring house in this village. Several people of both sexes were **assembled** in one of the apartments, and three or four others, with myself, were in another. At last came in a little elderly gentleman, pale, thin, with a solemn **countenance**, hooked nose, and hollow eyes. It was not long before we were summoned to attend in the apartment where he and the rest of the company were gathered. We went in and took our seats; the little elderly gentleman with the hooked nose prayed, and we all stood up. When he had finished, most of us sat down. The gentleman with the hooked nose then **muttered** certain **cabalistical** expressions which I was too much frightened to remember, but I recollect that at the conclusion I was given to understand that I was married to a young lady of the name of Frances Fairchild, whom I perceived standing by my side, and I hope in the course of a few months to have the pleasure of introducing to you as your daughter-in-law, which is a matter of some interest to the poor girl, who has neither father nor mother in the world...

I looked only for goodness of heart, an **ingenuous** and affectionate **disposition**, a good understanding, etc., and the character of my wife is too frank and **single-hearted** to suffer me to fear that I may be disappointed. I do myself wrong; I did not look for these nor any other qualities, but they trapped me before I was aware, and now I am married **in spite of myself**.

Thus the **current** of destiny carries us along. None but a mad man would swim against the stream, and none but a fool would exert himself to swim with it. The best way is to float quietly with the tide...

**Your affectionate son,
William**

为她的父母均已不在人世……

我只想找一个心地善良、纯朴温顺、善解人意的女人作妻子，这样的妻子性格坦率真诚，日后我不会后悔。我想错了，不是我在寻找具有这些品质的人，而是在我意识到之前就被这样的人捕获了。现在我只好身不由己地和人家结了婚。

因此，命运的洪流裹挟着我们向前。只有疯子才逆潮流而动，也只有傻子才极力追赶潮流。最好的就是什么也不做顺着潮流向前漂去……

您亲爱的儿子
威廉
1821年6月

单词解析 *Word Analysis*

melancholy ['melənkəli] *adj.* 忧郁的；悲伤的

例 He fixed me with those luminous, empty eyes and his melancholy smile.
他笑容忧郁地凝视着我，闪亮的眼睛里空无一物。

William Cullen Bryant to Sarah S. Bryant
威廉·卡伦·布莱恩特致萨拉·布莱恩特

assemble [əˈsembl] v. 聚集；集合
- All the students were asked to assemble in the main hall.
  全体学生获通知到大礼堂集合。

countenance [ˈkaʊntənəns] n. 表情；脸
- He met each inquiry with an impassive countenance.
  他面无表情地接受每一个盘问。

mutter [ˈmʌtə(r)] v. 嘀咕；嘟囔
- She just sat there muttering to herself.
  她坐在那儿独自唧唧咕咕的。

cabalistical [ˌkæbəˈlɪstɪkəl] adj. 神秘的，有神秘含义的
- Could you stop saying cabalistical words?
  你能别说神神道道的话了吗？

ingenuous [ɪnˈdʒenjuəs] adj. 坦率的；天真无邪的
- He found her charming, but perhaps just a shade too ingenuous for him.
  他觉得她很迷人，但对他来说可能又有点太过天真。

disposition [ˌdɪspəˈzɪʃn] n. 性情，性格
- The rides are unsuitable for people of a nervous disposition.
  骑马这一活动不适合天性易紧张的人。

single-hearted [ˈsɪŋglˈhɑːtɪd] adj. 诚实的，一心一意的
- He knew the simple single-hearted fidelity of his child.
  他十分了解他这个单纯朴实的孩子的孝心。

in spite of oneself 不由自主地
- We exclaimed at the good news in spite of ourselves.
  听到这个好消息，我们不由自主地欢呼。

current [ˈkʌrənt] n. 水流，潮流
- Birds use warm air currents to help their flight.
  鸟利用暖气流助飞。

语法知识点 *Grammar Points*

① At last came in a little elderly gentleman, pale, thin, with a solemn countenance, hooked nose, and hollow eyes.

这个句子中"at last"被提至句首,主语"gentleman"位于动词后,是一个倒装句,且为完全倒装。当表示时间、地点的副词被提至句首时,句子为完全倒装。

例 Here comes the boy who has a big dog.
那个养了只大狗的男孩走过来了。

② None but a mad man would swim against the stream, and none but a fool would exert himself to swim with it.

这个句子中"none but"表示"只有",同样的,其他否定词如"no、nothing、nobody、nowhere"等与"but"连用也可表示"只有、就是"。

例 He does nothing here but paring the potatoes.
他在这里什么也不做,除了削土豆。

经典名句 *Famous Classics*

1. Courage isn't having the strength to go on – it's going on when you don't have strength. — Napoleon Bonaparte
   勇气不是有力气坚持下去,而是没有力气时还坚持下去。——拿破仑·波拿巴

2. We need to accept that we won't always make the right decisions, that we'll screw up royally sometimes – understanding that failure is not the opposite of success. It's part of success. — Arianna Huffington, News Editor-in-Chief
   我们必须接受,我们无法总是做正确的决定,有时候大错特错——了解失败不是成功的相反,而是成功的一部分。——阿里安娜·赫芬顿(新闻主编)

3. The crisis of today is the joke of tomorrow. — H. G. Wells, Science Fiction Writer
   今天的危机会是明天的趣事。——赫伯特·乔治·威尔斯(科幻小说家)

4. Optimism is true moral courage. — Ernest Shackleton, Explorer
   乐观是精神上真正的勇气。——欧内斯特·沙克尔顿（探险家）

5. I knew that if I failed I wouldn't regret that, but I knew the one thing I might regret is not trying. — Jeff Bezos, Entrepreneur
   我知道我如果失败了，我不会后悔，但我知道我可能会后悔的是，没有去尝试。——杰佛瑞·贝佐斯（企业家）

6. To understand the heart and mind of a person, look not at what he has already achieved, but at what he aspires to do. — Khalil Gibran, Poet
   想了解一个人的内心世界，不要看他过去的成就，看他向往做什么。——哈里利·纪伯伦（诗人）

7. There is no pressure when you are making a dream come true. — Neymar, Soccer Player
   当你在圆梦时，你不会有压力。——内马尔（足球员）

8. You can overcome anything, if and only if you love something enough. — Lionel Messi, Soccer Player
   你可以克服任何事情，如果且只要你够热爱一件事。——利昂内尔·梅西（足球员）

读书笔记

38 George Gordon Byron to the Hon. Augusta Byron
乔治·戈登·拜伦致奥古斯塔·拜伦阁下

Harrow-on-the-Hill, 25 October 1804

My Dear Augusta,

In **compliance** with your wishes, as well as gratitude for your affectionate letter, I proceed as soon as possible to answer it; I am glad to hear that anybody gives a good account of me; but from the quarter you mention, I should imagine it was **exaggerated**. That you are unhappy, my dear Sister, makes me so also; were it in my power to relieve your sorrows you would soon recover your spirits; as it is, I sympathize better than you yourself expect. But really, after all (pardon me my dear Sister), I feel a little inclined to laugh at you, for love, in my humble opinion, is utter nonsense, a mere **jargon** of compliments, romance, and deceit; now, for my part, had I fifty mistresses, I should in the course of a fortnight, forget them all, and, if by any chance I ever recollected one, should laugh at it as a dream, and bless my stars, for delivering me from the hands of the little **mischievous** Blind God. Can't you drive this Cousin of ours out

亲爱的奥古斯塔：

应你的要求，也为了感谢你那封充满关怀的来信，我在尽可能快地给你回信；我很高兴，有人对我颇有赞誉；但从你提到的那些来看，这恐怕有所夸大了。我亲爱的姐姐，你不开心，我也不会开心；要是我有能力缓解你的痛苦的话，你早就精神焕发了；千真万确，我比你想象的还要同情你。但真的，归根结底（原谅我，亲爱的姐姐），我还是有点想要笑话你，因为在我看来，爱情什么都不是，只是充满了恭维、浪漫和欺骗的胡言乱语；对我而言，假如现在我有50个情妇的话，我会在不到两周的时间里把她们都忘掉的。就算我鬼使神差地记起了一个，也会把那人当作梦一场，一笑置之。并且感谢我的福星把我从那个爱恶作剧的小天神手中拯救出来。你就不能不要再想我们的这位表兄了

George Gordon Byron to the Hon. Augusta Byron

乔治·戈登·拜伦致奥古斯塔·拜伦阁下

of your pretty little head (for as to hearts I think they are out of the question), or if you are so far gone, why don't you give old L'Harpagon (I mean the General) the slip, and take up a trip to Scotland? You are now pretty near the Borders. Be sure to remember me to my formal Guardian Lord Carlisle, whose **magisterial** presence I have not been into for some years, nor have I any ambition to attain so great an honour. As to your favourite Lady Gertrude, I don't remember her; pray, is she handsome? I dare say she is, for although they are a disagreeable, formal, stiff generation, yet they have by no means plain persons. I remember Lady Cawdor was a sweet, pretty woman; pray, does your **sentimental** Gertrude resemble her? I have heard that the duchess of Rutland was handsome also, but we will say nothing about her temper, as I hate scandal.

Adieu, my pretty Sister, forgive my **levity**, write soon, and God bless you.

   I remain, your very affectionate
      Brother,
       Byron

吗？（从心底驱出，我认为不可能）或者，如果你已经走到了这一步，为什么不躲开老阿巴贡（我说的是将军），去苏格兰走一趟呢？你现在离边境是那么近。请一定要代我向我的正式监护人卡莱尔勋爵问好。我已经有几年没有受他严厉的管教了，我也不想再接受这份荣耀了。至于你最喜爱的格特鲁德小姐，我倒是记不得了；请问，她漂亮吗？我敢说她一定很漂亮，尽管她们那一辈人都惹人不快、拘谨刻板，但却绝非平庸之辈。我记得考德小姐就是一位漂亮可人的女士；请问，你那位感性的格特鲁德是否像她呢？我听说拉特兰公爵夫人也很端庄文雅，但是就不要谈她的性情了吧，因为我讨厌八卦丑闻。

再见了，我漂亮的姐姐，请原谅我的不甚庄重的言辞，并尽快回信。上帝保佑你。

    永远是你亲爱的弟弟
       拜伦
  1804年10月25日于哈罗山上

单词解析 Word Analysis

compliance [kəm'plaɪəns] *n.* 服从，听从

例 The company says it is in full compliance with US labor laws.
这家公司说自己严格遵守美国的各项劳工法。

exaggerate [ɪɡˈzædʒəreɪt] *v.* 夸张；夸大
- These figures exaggerate the loss of competitiveness.
  这些数字夸大了竞争力的丧失。

jargon [ˈdʒɑːɡən] *n.* 难懂的话；胡言乱语
- APEC seems be drowning in an ocean of jargon.
  亚太经合组织似乎为一大堆空洞的胡言乱语所淹没。

mischievous [ˈmɪstʃɪvəs] *adj.* 淘气的；恶作剧的
- The Foreign Office dismissed the story as mischievous and false.
  外交部驳斥该报道为恶意报道，不符合事实。

magisterial [ˌmædʒɪˈstɪəriəl] *adj.* 威严的；有权威的
- The Cambridge World History of Human Disease is a magisterial work.
  《剑桥世界人类疾病史》是一部权威著作。

sentimental [ˌsentɪˈmentl] *adj.* 多愁善感的；伤感的
- Our paintings and photographs are of sentimental value only.
  我们的画作和照片仅有纪念价值。

levity [ˈlevəti] *n.* 轻浮；轻率
- At the time, Arnold had disapproved of such levity.
  那时候的阿诺德对这种轻浮行为很看不惯。

语法知识点 *Grammar Points*

① I am glad to hear that anybody gives a good account of me.

这个句子中"be动词+（表示情绪的）形容词+ to do"是固定用法，表示"做某事令某人……"。

- He should be happy to hear that news.
  听到那个消息，他应该会很高兴。

② Were it in my power to relieve your sorrows you would soon recover your spirits.

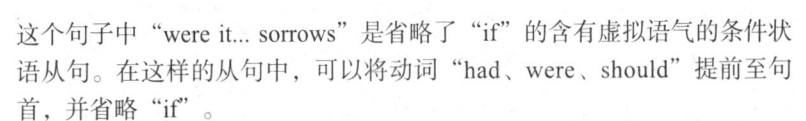

George Gordon Byron to the Hon. Augusta Byron
乔治·戈登·拜伦致奥古斯塔·拜伦阁下

这个句子中"were it... sorrows"是省略了"if"的含有虚拟语气的条件状语从句。在这样的从句中,可以将动词"had、were、should"提前至句首,并省略"if"。

例 Were there any person to help me, I could finish this work very soon.
要是有人来帮我,我就能很快完成这项工作了。

经典名句 Famous Classics

1. Nothing limits achievement like small thinking; nothing expands possibilities like unleashed imagination. — William Arthur Ward
想限制一个人的成就,莫过于自我设限的思考;想拓展可能,莫过于不加羁绊的想象。——西蒙·斯涅克

2. To one who has faith, no explanation is necessary. To one without faith, no explanation is possible. — Thomas Aquinas, Theologian
对于有信念的人,你不需做什么解释;对于没有信念的人,任何解释都没用。——托马斯·阿奎那(神学家)

3. The pessimist complains about the wind; the optimist expects it to change; the realist adjusts the sails. — William Arthur Ward, Scholar
悲观者抱怨风向,乐观者期待风向改变,务实的人调整帆布。——威廉·亚瑟·沃德(学者)

4. Faith is what gets you started. Hope is what keeps you going. Love is what brings you to the end. — Mother Mary Angelica
信念使你启身,希望让你坚持,爱带你到达终点。——安琪拉卡修女

5. Reason is our soul's left hand, faith her right, by these we reach divinity. — John Donne
逻辑是灵魂的左手,信念是它的右手,这两者可让我们到达神圣的境界。——约翰·多恩

6. Take pride in how far you've come. Have faith in how far you can go. But don't forget to enjoy the journey. — Michael Josephson, Ethics Speaker

对于你走完的路感到骄傲，对于你可以走多远感到自信，但不要忘记享受旅程。——麦克·乔瑟夫（伦理讲师）

7. Without faith, nothing is possible. With it, nothing is impossible.
   — Mary Bethune, Educator
   没有信念，没有事情是可能的。有了它，没有事情是不可能的。——玛丽·白求恩（教育家）

8. Faith is taking the first step even when you don't see the staircase.
   — Martin Luther King
   信念是踏上第一步，即便当你看不见楼梯时。——马丁·路德·金

读书笔记

39 George Gordon Byron to William Harness
乔治·戈登·拜伦致威廉·哈尼斯

8, St. James's Street, March 18, 1809

There was no necessity for your excuses: if you have time and **inclination** to write, "for what we receive, the Lord makes us thankful," –if I do not hear from you, I console myself with the idea that you are much more agreeably employed.

I send down to you by this post a certain **Satire** lately published, and **in return** for the three and six pence expenditure upon it, only beg that if you should guess the author, you will keep his name secret; at least for the present. London is full of the Duke's business. The Commons have been at it these last three nights, and are not yet come to a decision. I do not know if the affair will be brought before our House, unless in the shape of an **impeachment**. If it makes its appearance in a **debatable** form, I believe I shall be tempted to say something on the subject. –I am glad to hear you like Cambridge: firstly, because, to know that you are happy is pleasant to one who wishes you all

你无须辩解：如果你有时间和想法给我写信的话，"我们要为所得到的感激上帝"——如果我没有收到你的来信，我也会安慰自己，是你有更重要的事情要做。

我随信给你寄去了一首最近发表的讽刺诗，为此花了三先令六便士的邮费。看在邮费的份上，我只祈求你，如果猜到了作者是谁的话，不要告诉别人，至少现在不行。公爵的事情在伦敦已经人尽皆知。下议院这三个晚上一直在商议此事，但还没有决断。我不清楚这事会不会被提交到上议院去，除非是以弹劾的形式。如果会就此事进行辩论的话，我想我会对此发言的。——我很高兴听到你喜欢剑桥：因为，首先，对一个希望你得到人间所有快乐的人来说，是很乐意听到你心情很好的；其次，我钦佩你这种高尚的情感。我的母校于我就像是残酷的继母：

possible **sublunary** enjoyment; and, secondly, I admire the morality of the sentiment. **Alma Mater** was to me injusta noverca; and the old **beldam** only gave me my M.A. degree because she could not avoid it. –You know what a **farce** a noble **Cantab**. must perform.

I am going abroad, if possible, in the spring, and before I depart I am collecting the pictures of my most intimate schoolfellows; I have already a few, and shall want yours, or my cabinet will be incomplete. I have employed one of the first miniature painters of the day to take them, of course at my own expense, as I never allow my acquaintance to incur the least expenditure to gratify a **whim** of mine. To mention this may seem indelicate; but when I tell you a friend of ours first refused to sit, under the idea that he was to **disburse** on the occasion, you will see that it is necessary to state these **preliminaries** to prevent the **recurrence** of any similar mistake. I shall see you in time, and will carry you to the **limner**. It will be a tax on your patience for a week; but pray excuse it, as it is possible the **resemblance** may be the sole trace I shall be able to preserve of our past friendship and acquaintance. Just now it seems foolish enough, but in a few years, when some

这个恶毒的老太婆授予我文学硕士学位只是无可奈何之举。——你知道强迫一个高贵的剑桥大学的学生进行表演是怎样的一场闹剧。

我要出国了，可能就在春天。动身之前，我在收集我最亲密的校友的画像；我已经有几张了，还想要你的，不然我的橱柜是不完整的。我已经聘请了一位当今袖珍肖像画的一流画家来作画，当然是我付钱了，我从不会让好友为了满足我的古怪念头而花一分钱。提这个可能显得有些俗气，但要是我告诉你，有一个朋友以为这是要他出钱而不愿意坐下来时，你就会明白把这些提前说清楚是有必要的，这样可以避免同样的误会再次发生。我会及时去见你，然后带你去画师那里。这要一周的时间，可能需要你保持耐心。但是请原谅，这个肖像可能是保留我们昔日的友谊和情分的唯一办法了。现在这可能看起来有点傻，但是过几年，等到我们当中有人去世了，或者有人不得已天各一方时，活着的人能够在这些肖像里看到我们以前的自己、怀念逝者的想法、情感和激情，这是一种满足。但是这对你是太无聊了，所以晚安

of us are dead, and others are separated by **inevitable** circumstances, it will be a kind of satisfaction to retain in these images of the living the idea of our former selves, and to **contemplate** in the resemblances of the dead, all that remains of judgment, feeling, and a host of passions. But all this will be dull enough for you, and so good night; and to end my chapter, or rather my **homily**,

Believe me, my dear H., yours most affectionately.

吧,以此结束我这一封信,或者说教更准确一些。

相信我,亲爱的哈尼斯,你最亲爱的朋友。

1809年3月18日
于圣·詹姆斯街8号

单词解析 Word Analysis

inclination [ˌɪnklɪˈneɪʃn] *n.* 倾向;爱好

例 She had neither the time nor the inclination to help them.
她既没有时间也不愿意帮助他们。

satire [ˈsætaɪə(r)] *n.* 讽刺;讥讽;讽刺作品

例 The novel is a stinging satire on American politics.
这部小说是对美国政治的尖锐讽刺。

in return 作为报答

例 You pay regular premiums and in return the insurance company will pay out a lump sum.
你定期支付保险费,而保险公司则会一次性给你一笔钱作为回报。

impeachment [ɪmˈpiːtʃmənt] *n.* 弹劾;控告

例 There are grounds for impeachment.
存在弹劾的理由。

debatable [dɪˈbeɪtəbl] *adj.* 可争辩的;有争议的

例 Whether we can stay in this situation is debatable.
在这种情况下我们能否留下还很难说。

sublunary [sʌb'luːnərɪ] *adj.* 月下的，地上的
- It's hard to have all the sublunary happiness.
  很难拥有全部的尘世之乐。

Alma Mater [ˌælmə 'mɑːtə(r)] *n.* 母校
- He has fond feelings for his Alma Mater.
  他对自己的母校有着深厚的感情。

beldam ['beldəm] *n.* 恶婆；丑陋的老夫人
- I've never met such a beldam like her.
  我从来没有遇到过像她这样恶毒的妇人。

farce [fɑːs] *n.* 滑稽剧；笑剧
- The elections have been reduced to a farce.
  竞选演变为一场闹剧。

Cantab. *n.* 英国剑桥大学的学生或毕业生，英国剑桥的居民
- He is proud to be a Cantab.
  作为一名剑桥人，他很骄傲。

whim [wɪm] *n.* 心血来潮；一时的兴致
- We bought the house on a whim.
  我们一时冲动买了这所房子。

disburse [dɪs'bɜːs] *v.* （从资金中）支付，支出
- The aid will not be disbursed until next year.
  援助款到明年才会下拨。

preliminary [prɪ'lɪmɪnərɪ] *n.* 初步行动（或活动）；预备性措施
- I'll skip the usual preliminaries and come straight to the point.
  闲话少说，我就直接进入正题。

recurrence [rɪ'kʌrəns] *n.* 复回，重现
- Police are out in force to prevent a recurrence of the violence.
  警方出动大量警力防止暴力事件再次发生。

George Gordon Byron to William Harness

乔治·戈登·拜伦致威廉·哈尼斯

limner [ˈlɪmnə] *n.* 画匠，画家
- He wants to be the first class limner.
  他想成为顶级画家。

resemblance [rɪˈzembləns] *n.* 相似，形似；肖像
- The resemblance between the two signatures was remarkable.
  两个签名的相似之处非常明显。

inevitable [ɪnˈevɪtəbl] *adj.* 不可避免的；必然发生的
- A rise in the interest rates seems inevitable.
  提高利率似乎是不可避免的。

contemplate [ˈkɒntəmpleɪt] *v.* 考虑；思量
- For a time he contemplated a career as an army medical doctor.
  有段时间，他考虑去当军医。

homily [ˈhɒməli] *n.* （长篇）说教；讲道
- He launched into a homily on family relationships.
  他开始就家庭关系进行说教。

语法知识点 Grammar Points

① **If it makes its appearance in a debatable form, I believe I shall be tempted to say something on the subject.**

这个句子中"shall"与第一人称"I"连用，表示一个将来的动作。
- If he invites me, I shall accept his invitation immediately.
  如果他邀请我，我会立刻答应。

② **I have employed one of the first miniature painters of the day to take them, of course at my own expense, as I never allow my acquaintance to incur the least expenditure to gratify a whim of mine.**

这个句子中"one of"意为"其中之一"，用法为"one of + adj.最高级 + 可数名词复数"。
- She wants to be one of the best actresses in the world.
  她想成为世界上最好的女演员之一。

经典名句 Famous Classics

1. There is more to us than we know. If we can be made to see it, perhaps for the rest of our lives we will be unwilling to settle for less. — Kurt Hahn, Educator
我们的能力超出自己的想象,我们若能看见这个,可能往后的日子都不会和不理想妥协。——库尔特·汉(教育家)

2. One of the most beautiful qualities of true friendship is to understand and to be understood. — Lucius Annaeus Seneca, Philosopher
真友谊最美的一个特质是了解和被了解。——卢修斯·阿纳乌斯·塞内卡(哲学家)

3. False friendship, like the ivy, decays and ruins the walls it embraces; but true friendship gives new life and animation to the object it supports. — Richard Burton, Actor
不好的友谊像藤蔓,腐烂毁坏它所攀附的墙壁,但真正的友谊,会将新生命及活力注入它所支持的对象。——理查德·波顿(演员)

3. Joyfulness keeps the heart and face young. A good laugh makes us better friends with ourselves and everybody around us. — Orison Marden, Writer
愉快让内心及面容保持年轻。成为一个有趣的人,使我们更喜欢自己,也和周遭的人成为更好的朋友。——奥里森·马登(作家)

4. There are no regrets in life, just lessons. — Jennifer Aniston, Actress
人生中没有后悔,只有教训。——珍妮佛·安妮斯顿(演员)

5. Friendship that flows from the heart cannot be frozen by adversity, as the water that flows from the spring cannot congeal in winter. — James Fenimore Cooper, Novelist
出自真心的友谊不会因逆境而冻结,如同泉水不会在冬天里结冻。——詹姆士·菲尼莫尔·库柏(小说家)

6. I will destroy my enemies by converting them to friends. — Moses Maimonides, Jewish Philosopher

我将借由把敌人变为朋友来消灭我的敌人。——摩西·迈蒙尼德（犹太哲学家）

7. The shifts of fortune test the reliability of friends. — Marcus Tullius Cicero, Roman Philosopher
命运的转变会测试朋友的可靠度。——西塞罗（罗马哲学家）

8. Prosperity makes friends; adversity tries them. — Publilius Syrus, Latin Writer of Maxims
兴盛结交朋友，逆境考验他们。——普布里利亚·西鲁斯（拉丁格言家）

读书笔记

读书笔记